Worthless No More

Mishell Wolff

Copyright © 2017 by Mishell Wolff

All Rights Reserved

No part of this publication may be reproduced, distributed, or transmitted in any form or by any means, stored in a database or retrieval system, without the prior written permission of the author/publisher.

This edition published by Mishell Wolff

Cover Design: Geoff Siler, Boomslang Studios

Cover Photo: Mishell Wolff

Cover Model: Aleigh Wolff

Printed in the United States of America

For readers age 14 years and older.

For my wonderful husband and kids,
Thank you for the amazing life we have.

Table of Contents

Preface 9

Chapter One 11

Chapter Two 23

Chapter Three 31

Chapter Four 36

Chapter Five 40

Chapter Six 48

Chapter Seven 54

Chapter Eight 59

Chapter Nine 66

Chapter Ten 72

Chapter Eleven 77

Chapter Twelve 83

Chapter Thirteen 89

Chapter Fourteen 96

Chapter Fifteen 102

Chapter Sixteen 111

Chapter Seventeen 121

Chapter Eighteen 130

Chapter Nineteen 134

Chapter Twenty 140

Chapter Twenty-One 145

Chapter Twenty-Two 148

Chapter Twenty-Three 156

Chapter Twenty-Four 163

Chapter Twenty-Five 178

Chapter Twenty-Six 184

Chapter Twenty-Seven 193

Chapter Twenty-Eight 200

Chapter Twenty-Nine 209

Chapter Thirty 216

Chapter Thirty-One 219

Chapter Thirty-Two 224

Chapter Thirty-Three 231

Epilogue 234

Acknowledgements 235

About the Author 236

Preface

This is my story, from my perspective. This is how I remember the events and people that shaped my life. Friends and family members who observed various parts of my life may have a different perspective, but that is their story to tell, not mine.

If you have experienced any kind of abuse my story may trigger strong emotions or intense reactions. In that case, I hope that you can read my story and find healing for your own. If you need to talk to someone find a counselor, a friend or a law enforcement officer.

Here are phone numbers for 24-hour help:
Sexual Assault Hotline 1-800-656-4673
Suicide Hotline 1-800-273-8255
Domestic Violence Hotline 1-800-799-SAFE (7233)

Chapter One

The last few minutes of my freshman year of high school were crawling by. The second hand on the clock was moving as slow as molasses in winter. The classroom was alive with nonstop chattering about summer plans. Everyone was anxiously waiting for the final bell to ring, to be released from another year of education into the freedom that summer brings.

My summer would not be the same as my classmates, they would have fun and freedom, while I would have chores and boredom. The only freedom I'd have would be when my sister and I were allowed to attend youth group activities with our church.

With another school year over, I was one year closer to being able to get away from my house, go to college and get a job that would finally make my parents proud of me and maybe, finally, earn their love. In the meantime, I was stuck in my miserable life with their miserable expectations.

They expected me to get up early to wake my dad because he required a human alarm clock, me. Then I would have to help with breakfast. It would be up to me to see to it that my thirteen-year-old sister, Stefyni (pronounced Stephanie), and my eleven-year-old brother, Keeth, did chores, got along, had lunch, didn't fight and didn't watch television all day. Then, in the evening I would make dinner for the three of us, and maybe my mom, if she chose to eat with us. At the expected time, I would make sure that we went to bed after showers and teeth brushing. That would be a typical day in my life.

At some point after falling asleep, my dad would come in to my room and wake me up. It was a familiar routine after living with my dad again for the past four years.

Sometime after I finished for the day, had everything put away and was sound asleep, enjoying a world of dreams, my dad would put his face right next to mine as I slept on the top bunk. He would tell me that he was hungry. I would have to get up and make dinner for him. It didn't matter that we had eaten hours ago, or that it was midnight or later. He would be hungry and apparently unable to warm his own left overs. I would get up and make his dinner because that's what he expected. We kids, especially me, were there to be at his beck and call at any hour. If I did what he wanted, I could just go back to bed, if I didn't do it, I'd be yelled at, called names and maybe beaten with his three-foot-long wooden baseboard that he kept for just that purpose.

My parents' love for me was conditional. They only loved me when I did their bidding, followed their rules, and was miserable. I have memories about this, going back as young as I can remember; being told to stop crying unless I wanted something to cry about, or to go outside so that I wouldn't bother them.

When I was six years old I realized that my dad didn't love me. It was the summer just after first grade when my parents separated and my mom took the three of us and my older sister to live in a run-down triplex in a part of town known for being rough. As a child, I didn't understand that it was my parents' problem to solve. I firmly believed that if my dad loved my siblings and me, he would have worked things out with my mom and let us stay there. From that summer until halfway through sixth grade I wanted them back together, because I thought my dad would love me then. I was wrong, living with him didn't change how he treated us.

At nine-years old I had pneumonia for the third time in about ten months. The doctor told my mom that she shouldn't smoke in the house because it just made my illnesses more frequent. On the way home from the doctor that day my mom ranted. "Who the hell does that doctor think he is? Telling me where I can and cannot smoke! It's my damn house and if I want to smoke inside my own house, I damn well will!" That was the moment I knew that my mom didn't love me.

In a word, I felt worthless. How could I feel any other way, when my own parents didn't love me?

Finally, the bell rang and summer was upon us. The other students talked excitedly as they rushed through the doors into the mid-June sunshine welcoming us outside, while I trudged to the bus and on towards the misery that awaited me at home.

I leaned my head against the warm window of the school bus watching the scenery change from vineyards to orchards to pasture. I was reminded as person after person exited the bus and I was soon left alone, that my summer would be like that too, lonely. Friends were not allowed at our house and we were only allowed twenty minutes of phone time each hour so endless phone calls to friends was also out of the question, leaving my social life to consist of church on Sundays and youth group on Wednesdays, as well as whatever youth activities our church sponsored and my parents allowed me to attend.

There was a youth activity coming up on Tuesday, a skate night at the roller skating rink. I looked forward to those few times to be away from my parents' watchful, judgmental eyes. Being with the youth group was a bright spot in my otherwise dismal life.

The days dragged by as I waited for the skate night. When Tuesday arrived, I made sure that all the chores were done, the house was clean, dishwasher loaded, and everybody fed so that my parents wouldn't change their mind and not allow me to go.

The skating rink was electric when Stefyni and I walked in. Music was pumping through the speakers hung at odd angles from walls, the main lights were dim and the colorful party lights danced around the walls and floor of the rink. People were skating, laughing and talking on the skate floor as well as in the snack bar and table area. We were in for a good night away from home.

I was skating and having a great time with friends when I heard the DJ announce, "Hey guys and gals, it's time to find that someone special for a couple's skate. So, find someone who makes your heart beat a little faster, grab their hand and enjoy some time together."

Even on Christian night, they had a couple's skate. Just as the announcement ended this exceptionally good looking guy, that I had been watching, skated by me.

"Would you like to skate with me?" he asked with a smile that lit up his whole face as he held his hand out to me.

Blushing, I responded, "Yes."

I couldn't believe that he asked me to skate with him. Nobody ever noticed me, I was just a plain, skinny girl, but here was this good-looking guy holding out his hand to me. I reached out, laced my fingers between his, and began skating beside him, my head spinning and my heart racing.

"I'm Jay." He introduced himself, leaning close to my ear.

"I'm Mishell." I replied over the music. My hand was starting to sweat. I was so nervous; I didn't want to embarrass myself in front of him.

The music played, but all I could focus on was Jay. He asked questions about me as we skated laps around the floor. He seemed to honestly want to know about me. I answered all his questions and asked a few of my own. He fascinated me. He would be a senior when school started again, he had a driver's license and a job. He seemed like a dream come true. When the couple's skate ended, he didn't release my hand and I wasn't about to let go. We kept skating and talking until the end of the session. It was amazing. This attractive guy was paying attention to me, talking to me and making me feel special.

When the session was over, Stefyni, walked up while stuffing the laces into her skates, and asked, "Have you seen Dustin? We have to get home soon and I can't find him anywhere!" Dustin was a friend of ours that my mom trusted to give us rides to church and activities when she was too tired or sick.

"I haven't seen him. What time is it?" I questioned a little worried.

Stefyni checked her watch, "9:40. We're gonna be late!"

"I don't wanna get home late. I'll get grounded again. I'll call and let Ma know." I started to dig for change to use the pay phone. I came up a few cents short. "Stef, do you have any change? I don't have enough for a long-distance call."

Stefyni began to check for change. We scrounged up what we thought would be enough for the call then went to the pay phone hanging on the wall across from the skate return counter. Just as I picked up the receiver, Dustin came up behind us.

"Hey," He tapped Stefyni's shoulder. "You guys ready to go?" He didn't even notice that we were freaking out.

I smiled and placed the receiver back on its cradle. "Let's go. I don't want to be late!"

"Oh, by the way, I'm taking Jay home too." He added nonchalantly.

The four of us, Stefyni, Dustin, Jay and I, hurried to Dustin's tiny, blue car and climbed in. I squeezed behind the passenger seat into the back. Surprisingly, Jay got in behind the driver's seat. Stefyni took the front seat. When Dustin started the engine, the dashboard clock said 9:48.

"You have twelve minutes to get us home. How fast are you?" Stefyni wanted to know.

"Don't worry," Dustin replied, backing out of the parking spot. "I haven't gotten you home late yet. I'm not about to start tonight." He then pulled onto the street, heading towards the freeway.

Dustin sped towards our house while I sat in the back seat panicking because we were going to get home late. I didn't want to get yelled at; we should have called to let my mom know we'd be late. I mentally willed Dustin to drive faster and get us home on time. That meant we needed enough time to walk up the hundred-yard driveway and be in the house by 10 o'clock.

When Dustin pulled into our driveway, the dashboard clock read 10:03. It was too late. We would be grounded. No escaping to church for at least two weeks. My parents would yell at me and blame it all on me. I didn't want to deal with that. It didn't matter if it was three minutes late or three hours late, late was late and I would be in trouble. One time I was two minutes late getting home and I was grounded for two weeks, so I was certain of the outcome for this.

"Since we're gonna get busted anyway," I began hesitantly, "what if we just stayed out later? I mean, we might as well make it worthwhile to be grounded. Right, Stef? Let's have some fun. What'd'ya say Dustin? Wanna go for a drive?" I finished. I couldn't believe the words actually came out of my mouth, but I knew I would be grounded anyway, so what did it matter? My parents didn't care about me, so why not make the punishment worthwhile?

"Yes!" Stef agreed, surprising me.

Dustin shrugged his shoulders, backed the car out of the driveway and took off down the street. "So, where are we going?"

"I don't know; I've never done something like this before. What do you do out this late?" I questioned.

Jay slid his arm over my shoulders. "We could go park somewhere in the country."

"And just what are Stef and I supposed to do while we're parked? I know what you plan on doing."

"Let's just drive around." I suggested.

Jay scooted closer to me in the backseat and placed his arm across my shoulders. Then he leaned close to my ear, whispering "Are you sure you don't want to go park? We could get to know each other better." I couldn't see his face, but I could sense his eagerness.

I knew what Jay meant by parking; he wanted to make out with me. It was flattering, but I didn't know him well enough yet to do that. We had only just met a few hours earlier. The attention he was giving me was definitely a welcome difference to the yelling I usually received from my parents and the feeling of invisibility I usually experienced at school. It felt good to be wanted.

Dustin backed out of the driveway and drove away from our house talking with Stefyni in the front seat, while Jay I continued to talk in the back seat. He was constantly touching me; resting his hand on my knee, putting his arm around my shoulders, his fingers intertwined with mine. I couldn't stop smiling, enjoying this positive attention, realizing that I craved the good feelings it brought.

Eventually we arrived at a marina. The reflection of the moon on the water was beautiful. I asked if we could get out and walk for a bit. It was a warm, comfortable night as we walked along the river. Dustin and Stefyni walked ahead, leaving Jay and I alone.

We walked hand in hand in silence. I could barely enjoy the peaceful, idyllic surroundings because my thoughts were racing and my heart was pounding in my ears. I would be in trouble when we got home, but the butterflies in my stomach made it seem like it wouldn't be so bad.

While we walked, I glanced sideways at Jay to take in the entire package with the backdrop of the moon reflected in the still water of the river. He was tall, well a lot of people were tall to my five-foot-two-inch height, and he had deep brown eyes I could see in the dim moonlight, and black hair. On the outside, he was a great package and he was talking to me! He was walking with me! He was holding my hand! I was one lucky girl!

When Dustin and Stefyni were so far ahead of us they were just silhouettes in the dark, Jay stopped walking and faced me taking my other hand in his as well. I looked up as he looked down, our eyes meeting, locking onto one another. It seemed he could see right into me: that he could know what I was thinking. He smiled. My insides exploded with excitement. It was too much for me to take in and I wanted to cry, but I refused to make myself look so childish in front of Jay.

"I think I'm starting to like you." He whispered.

I blushed and looked away, smiling. This couldn't be happening. This cute, Christian guy liked me. Nervously, I looked back up, into his eyes, "I like you, too."

I knew it was happening so quickly, but he liked me. He was cute. He went to church. He was a Christian. He was listening to me when we talked. He made me feel important, like I mattered. I needed to feel accepted and good enough.

He leaned towards me and kissed me lightly on the lips. It surprised me. His lips were soft and smooth and perfect. His kiss was warm and sweet, I wanted it to continue.

Just then Dustin and Stefyni walked back, interrupting us. "Hey," Stefyni began "let's drive past our house now. If the lights are out, we can go in because that means Daddy will be asleep and won't know how late we are."

I shrugged my shoulders in agreement and we walked towards Dustin's car. We each climbed into the same position as before, except that I sat so close to Jay this time that my leg was resting against his leg, skin to skin. He had his arm around my shoulder and his other hand rested on my thigh. It was a little higher on my leg than I was comfortable with, but

I didn't want to make him mad by saying something, so I let it go and chalked it up to the fact that he liked me.

We talked throughout the fifteen-minute drive towards our house. Dustin slowed the car down as we drew near the house. We looked for the lights to be off, however they were still on.

"Shoot! He's still downstairs. It's already after 11:00. We're going to be in so much trouble. I'm not ready for that. Let's keep going, Dustin."

Stefyni agreed with me and Jay patted my shoulder reassuringly. I guess he thought I made a good decision.

We drove for another twenty minutes or so before Dustin asked, "Are you ready to go home now?"

"Please, Mishell." Stefyni begged. "We're gonna get beat for sure!"

"Let's check the light again. If it's off we'll go in, if it's on we keep driving. Alright, Dustin?"

"Fine with me. Stef, is that okay with you?

Stefyni released an exasperated sigh before answering, "Fine!"

Driving back towards our house, Jay leaned close to me, whispering in my ear. His warm breath cascaded down my neck, giving me chills, exciting me. Could he be having the same reaction to me? Could he possibly have the same butterfly feeling in the pit of his stomach? I doubted that I was capable of doing that to anybody, but hoped for it all the same.

Dustin slowed the car as we neared my house again, this time pulling into the driveway next door to have a better view of the lights. They were still on, that meant my dad was still downstairs. It was nearing midnight as Dustin backed out and drove off again.

"Where to now?" he asked.

"Let's just drive," Stefyni replied.

"Let's find a dark, quiet country road to park on." Jay suggested, echoing his earlier request.

"Drive it is then." Dustin acquiesced to Stefyni. I was silently relieved; I still wasn't ready to park with Jay.

We drove, talking together the entire time. I was snuggled up to Jay in the back seat, getting a little less uncomfortable with his attention; I was enjoying being the center of his attention. After driving for quite some time, at least an hour, Jay finally convinced Dustin to find a quiet, dark spot to park. Dustin stopped near a cherry orchard and he and Stefyni got out of the car to walk around in the cool, comfortable late night air, while Jay and I stayed put in the back seat.

Jay leaned in and kissed me. "Have you ever made out with anyone before?"

"No." Shy, embarrassed and refusing to look him in the eye.

"I'll teach you?" With that he placed one finger under my chin, tilting my face up towards his, wrapped his other arm around me, and kissed me long and passionately. I couldn't breathe; if the world ended right then I would die the happiest I had ever been. I had never felt so wanted and accepted as in that moment.

As we continued kissing, I relaxed, getting comfortable. Apparently so was Jay as his hands began to roam over my body. I wasn't entirely comfortable when his hand went a little too high up my thigh, under the hem of my shorts. He gave me the chills kissing down my neck and his hand paused on the front of my shirt, I enjoyed kissing him and tolerated his roaming hands. I wouldn't stop him and risk him not liking me anymore. Even so, I was more than a little relieved when Dustin and Stefyni came back to the car.

Stefyni opened the passenger side door and climbed in, looking tired. "I'm exhausted. We need to go home."

"Alright." I agreed, pulling away from Jay's embrace, but still close enough for physical contact with him.

As the four of us drove back to my house, Jay leaned close and whispered in my ear. "Will you be my girlfriend?"

I was beyond shocked. This guy, who just happened to be tall, dark and handsome, as well as a great kisser, wanted me to be his girlfriend. Somebody thought I was worth the time and effort to be a girlfriend. It didn't matter anymore that my mom and dad didn't love or care about me; this guy did. He accepted me for me. I hadn't done anything spectacular to get his attention, but he liked me. I wouldn't let that slip away.

"Yes! I'd love to be your girlfriend!" I exclaimed. When Stefyni heard that she turned around in her seat and rolled her eyes. Dustin kept his eyes forward as he continued to drive toward our house.

Not too long after I officially became Jay's girlfriend, Dustin pulled his car into our driveway. I leaned over and gave Jay a quick hug and kiss on the lips as Stefyni extricated herself from the front seat. I climbed out after her and Jay followed. He pulled me in to a bear hug as though he didn't want to let me go. I melted into his chest, allowing his strong arms to envelop me. He kissed me one more time as Stefyni pulled my arm to go in. Jay climbed in the front seat as we reached the gate. Both of us turned to wave goodbye. "Thanks for the ride" we said in unison.

Dustin sat parked in his car, shining his headlights down the long dark, driveway, illuminating our walk to the house and imminent doom. The living room lights were still on. Our only hope was that our dad would be asleep on the couch and we would be able to sneak in without him knowing how late it was.

We rounded the corner of the house to the door closest to our bedroom and farthest from the living room where my dad was no doubt sleeping on the couch. I opened the door as quietly as possible and Stefyni closed it just the same. As we tiptoed across the kitchen to our bedroom and hopefully safety, I noticed the clock on the microwave said 2:19. We paused at the end of the counter to look down the hall, willing our dad to be asleep on the couch. He was there, his eyes closed, breathing deeply.

We risked walking across the hall to our room, but it was too late. Without opening his eyes our dad demanded, "Who's that trying to sneak in at two o'clock in the morning? Weren't you supposed to be home at ten? Your mother is out looking for you! She's been driving around for the past three hours. Go to your room and wait."

Trembling, we did as he demanded, dread filling my heart and mind.

Chapter Two

We changed into pajamas in silence. I was terrified of what was going to happen. My dad was angry, and he would blame and punish me for staying out so late. It didn't matter though because it would have been the same consequence even if we had come in the first time we came home. However, my mom being out driving around was something I hadn't anticipated. Maybe my mom did care about me and wanted to make sure I was safe.

We waited in silence. The butterflies in my stomach returned, reminding me that I was special to someone, reminding me that whatever punishment I received was worth it because I met Jay. Not just because I had met Jay, because I made out with Jay and I was his girlfriend now.

About twenty minutes later, Stefyni and I were still waiting in silence in our bedroom when we heard my mom walk in the door in the living room. My dad moaned when he raised himself off the couch and fell in step beside her, walking down the hall to our bedroom.

"Where the hell have you been?" he began.

Before either of us could answer, my mom started in, "Do you know that I've been out driving around with the pastor for the past few hours. What do you think he thinks about you when he knows the two of you left the skating rink with two boys and they didn't go home either? We checked with their parents! I'll tell you what he thinks! He thinks that I raised daughters who run off with boys and does God knows what! I can't believe you put me in this situation. You've completely embarrassed me. I don't know how I'm ever going to go back to that church with daughters like you! I don't know how I can ever show my face there again! What they'll think of me! My daughters staying out until the wee hours of the morning with two boys!"

"When hell freezes over is when they'll go back to that church. If they're just going to screw every Tom, Dick and Harry there, they can just stay home! I'll be God damned if you two will have any freedom this summer! I'm not surprised about Mishell, but Stefyni, my favorite! You couldn't talk some sense into shit for brains over there? Get your sorry asses in bed. You're grounded for the rest of the summer!"

My parents left the room quietly, my mom shaking her head. Stefyni slipped onto the bottom bunk and laid down without saying a word.

I willed myself not to cry in front of my parents or Stefyni, refusing to give them the satisfaction. I climbed the ladder up to my bunk, slid between the sheets then curled into a ball on my left side. I snuggled in under the blanket and pulled my light green baby-blanket up to my face and sobbed into the familiar fabric which I often used to stifle my tears.

It didn't matter how many times they got mad or yelled at me and called me names, each time they did it hurt as though it was the first time they made me feel unimportant and unloved. Then my dad had thrown in the part about Stefyni being his favorite. Did he have to add that? He might as well have just straight said that I wasn't good enough for him. That I needed to be better and work harder at being good.

My sobs quieted and I took the blanket away from my face, wiping away the final tears. Next to me on the bed was my Bible. At that moment, I didn't even know if God loved me, I had let Him down tonight. After all, I had let Jay touch me in places he shouldn't have. I just didn't want to lose him already. He was so cute and seemed to like me. It was nice to be noticed. I thoroughly enjoyed the butterflies in the stomach feeling I had experienced earlier with him. I longed for the acceptance he offered. He was a Christian after all. God should be okay with that. I decided to talk to Jay later about where his hands were going, if we kissed again. I smiled at the thought of kissing him again. I vowed to be good with Jay, so that God would still love me.

I laid in bed thinking about my mom and what I had learned from her about God's love and acceptance. I learned from her that if we follow all God's rules, He'll love us and allow us into heaven when we died. She was a religious freak and wanted her kids to get into heaven by following God's rules, one of which was to attend church, so I was confident we'd be back there on Sunday, even though my dad said no church. My emotions were a roller coaster as I tried to sleep, fluctuating between hurt, anger, joy, pain, and excitement until sleep claimed my exhausted mind.

My dad was in my face before the sun was up the next morning. "Shit for brains, time to get up."

I slowly opened my eyes to see my dad's face. "You need to get the eggs from the wash-porch fridge. Think you can handle that?" he continued without waiting for me to respond. "Then start cutting bread for toast. Don't screw up!" With that he walked out of my bedroom into the kitchen and began getting the skillet out. I wondered how he woke up without me, did he even have an alarm clock?

The sky outside my window was just turning to dawn. I was exhausted. Throwing my blanket off, I slid off the side of my bunk to the floor. Stefyni was waking up too. I trudged down the hall, through the living room onto the wash porch to get the eggs out of that refrigerator. It was an old one with a latching door. When I closed it I remembered to make sure it latched to keep from being yelled at later. I took the egg carton back to the kitchen.

"I need four eggs." I heard as soon as I returned to the kitchen. I hadn't even had chance to go to the bathroom yet, but I knew better than to tell him I needed to do that.

I took two eggs from each end of the carton to keep the rest balanced in the center, exactly how he'd taught me to do it. I'd been called names and belittled for not doing it correctly plenty of times before. I placed the carton in the refrigerator in the kitchen, on the middle shelf to the left. Making sure I did everything just right would keep me from a verbal lashing.

"Put them here." He said, pointing to the tile counter next to the stove where he stood. I obeyed, being careful not to drop them. "Cut the bread and make the toast. One slice for each of you." I did as he instructed.

After breakfast my dad told my brother, sister and I that he was leaving. He gave us a list of things to get done and reminded us that we were grounded and that we couldn't leave our bedroom except to do chores.

The night before Jay and I had exchanged phone numbers. While I waited for my dad to leave, I silently debated if I should call him. Would I look too desperate calling him so soon? Was he even interested in me or did he just want a make out session? He did ask me to be his girlfriend, but what did that mean? I'd never been a girlfriend before. Would my dad catch me on the phone and ground me for even longer or never let me go back to church again? I desperately wanted to talk to him, but didn't want to be in any more trouble. I still didn't know how long I was grounded for; how long it would be before I could go to church and see him again. When could I tell my mom that Jay was my boyfriend? I didn't know why life had to be so difficult and why my parents couldn't just love me. I had screwed up the night before and many other times, but shouldn't they love me anyway? Isn't that how parents were supposed to be, all about unconditional love? It felt like I had to earn their love and acceptance and the older I got, the harder it was to earn.

After much internal strife, I decided to call Jay. I was his girlfriend after all and I should be able to call him without looking desperate. I waited for a while after my dad left to be sure he was gone, I went to the yellow, rotary phone hanging on the cabinet across from my bedroom door. I looked at the paper that had his number scribbled on it from the night before and dialed. I actually had to dial and wait for the dial to get back into place after each number. It rang and someone answered the phone.

"Hello." A girl answered.
"Hello, is Jay there?" I was so nervous; my hand was sweating and trembling as I gripped the receiver.
"Just a second," to me, then "Jay, some chick's on the phone for you!" I heard her say as she put the phone down.

I didn't have to wait too long for him to get on the phone. We talked a little about what happened to me when I got home last night. He told me that he wanted to see me again. Right then. He was going to have his brother drive him over.

"If I get caught with you guys here, I'll be in even more trouble."
"Are your parents home right now?"
"Well, no, but I don't know when my dad will get back. My mom gets home about 4:00."
"Then we'll come right now. See you in fifteen minutes." And with that he hung up.

I didn't know what to think or feel. I was ecstatic that he wanted to see me again, but I was petrified for him to come over. If my dad ever found out that he came to our house after staying out with him half the night, he would kill me, but it was worth the risk. I really liked him, and if Jay found out how strict my dad was, he'd probably be scared off and never want to see me again.

    I told Stefyni that Jay and his brother were on their way over. She warned me about how much trouble I would be in if I got caught. That was pointless, she didn't need to say anything; my heart was pounding with fear and excitement. My emotions were a giant contradiction.

    About ten minutes later, I checked myself in the bathroom mirror, I wanted to be cute. I looked how I normally did; long straight brown hair, half pulled up in a barrette and no makeup. It was exactly how I had looked the night before when he asked me to be his girlfriend. I still couldn't get over the fact that I, Mishell Allen, was Jay's girlfriend. Being someone's girlfriend was the best thing to happen to me. My parents, who were supposed to love me didn't, but being Jay's girlfriend meant that he chose me. That made me special to at least one person.

    A wall of heat hit me as I walked outside to peek down the driveway. There he was, leaning against his brother's car wearing black shorts and a white tank top that showed off his well-defined, tan arms. My heart skipped a beat and it was all I could do to walk down the driveway instead of run, but I wanted to be cool, calm and collected, at least outwardly because it seemed I was flying and everything was fireworks inside of me.

    When I got to the wire gate that closed our driveway from the street, Jay was waiting just on the other side. I unlocked the padlock, opened the gate and he enveloped me in his arms. His five-foot-ten-inch height to my five foot two inches, meant that when he hugged me I was completely surrounded by him. His brother sat in the car, where he stayed with the windows down, the entire time they were there.

"We have to stay down here," I explained. "My dad won't let us bring people in the house and he'll know someone was here if you come in."

"As long as I get to see you we can stay here." Then he kissed me.

Fireworks exploded in my heart. My stomach was full of butterflies and doing flip-flops. My mind was racing. He must really like me to come to my house. My dad would yell if he caught me with somebody over, especially while I was grounded, yet at that moment, standing at the end of my driveway, wrapped in Jay's arms, I didn't care what might happen if I got caught with him at my house. All that mattered was that Jay had his arms around me and I was on fire inside.

Jay and his brother didn't stay long; we thought I had better chances of being allowed to date him if he didn't get caught being at my house when he wasn't supposed to be there. He gave me a sweet kiss and hug before he left. I walked back to the house on cloud nine. It didn't even matter that I still had a ton of chores to do; someone chose me as his girlfriend. I was important to someone. Jay accepted me in a way my parents never had and I needed that.

Stefyni, Keeth and I spent the rest of the day doing chores to keep from getting yelled at later. We had dishes to wash and put in the dishwasher. We had to scrub the toilet, tub and bathroom sink, vacuum and mop the house. Our parents left us with quite a list of chores that morning to be completed before our mom came home. We accomplished all of them to her satisfaction. We spent the rest of the day in our bedrooms.

When my mom came home Stefyni and I convinced her that we should be allowed to go to church on Sunday. We tried for youth group that night, but failed, it was too soon. I decided to tell her about Jay, at least part of it. I told her I had met a guy skating the night before and that he asked me to be his girlfriend. She said she was happy for me, although I couldn't tell if she really was or not. Very often I had seen her say one thing to a person only to get away from them and say something entirely different and usually judgmental, but if I was going to be Jay's girlfriend I would need her on my side to go places with him.

I told my mom that Jay went to church with us and that she could meet him on Sunday. She reminded me that I couldn't go on an actual date until I was fifteen. I wasn't going to argue about that since my birthday was six weeks away and I'd probably be grounded for most of that time.

At least I would be able to see Jay at church on Sundays. Most of the punishment didn't seem too extreme. We were only allowed twenty minutes of phone time per day to begin with and nobody ever came over, so being grounded from the phone and having friends over wasn't that big of a deal. The most difficult part to deal with was not being able to attend youth group. That was an escape that I looked forward to each week; time out of the judgmental eye of my parents. A time when it was just friends, God and me.

Chapter Three

When I was in first grade I started bugging my mom to take me to church. I drew pictures of what I imagined heaven and God to look like. I wished I could go there. Heaven seemed like an amazing, peaceful place. I longed for a place where there was no fighting or yelling and I believed Heaven was that place. I knew I'd have to die to get to Heaven, and at six-years-old I didn't want to die. I assumed church would be a peaceful place, very similar to heaven.

When I was eight years old my mom finally took us to the church that my aunt attended. I think we went more because my aunt invited us than that I had been begging to go. It didn't matter to me why we finally went to church; I was excited to go. That church had a place just for kids to go while the adults went to the main service. It was called Kids of the Kingdom. I don't know what I expected when I walked into that large crowded room with my sister, but what I saw wasn't it.

At the front of the room was a large man with a beard in front of a puppet stage draped with navy blue fabric. He was singing, leading the kids. There were child size chairs in rows facing the man at the front, most of the chairs were already filled with children. A nice woman came to help my sister and I find seats, we ended up getting separated. When I sat down next to a kid I didn't know, I burst into tears. I was frightened and alone in a new situation.

The large man at the front of the room noticed me and saw that I was crying. I think the whole room noticed that I was crying, sobbing actually. The loud choking kind of sobs with alligator tears running down my cheeks. He walked over to me, knelt down beside me and introduced himself.

"Hi! I'm Pastor Tim. Can you turn that frown upside down?"

I shook my head from side to side, still crying.

"Why are you so sad?"

"I. Want. My. Sister." I managed to get out between sobs.

Almost as soon as the words were out of my mouth a chair was brought next to me and my sister was sitting beside me. With my sister beside me, I enjoyed the rest of Kids of the Kingdom that morning. We sang songs, Pastor Tim did magic and taught us about God and Jesus. I left there that morning with a feeling of peace that I had never experienced before. On the drive home I begged my mom to go back the next Sunday.

We did go back the next Sunday, and the one after that and the next until we were attending that church every Sunday. I didn't cry anymore when I attended Kids of the Kingdom. I was extremely comfortable there and enjoyed learning about Jesus.

The more I learned the more I longed to know. I was a sponge soaking in all I could about the Lord. His loving kindness, His steadfastness, His healing powers. The peace was overwhelming. I relished the feeling of complete love and peace that I felt at church.

On Easter Sunday 1983, I accepted the fact that I needed Jesus to be the Lord of my life and that would get me into Heaven. I went home ecstatic that God loved me and I was part of the family of God. I learned over the next few months that God is like a father to those who love Him. That He loves us the way a parent loves their child. As a young child, I believed this literally, not figuratively.

I believed that God would only love me when I was being good and following His rules. My parents had a ton of rules that I had to follow for them to love me, so it had to be the same with God. I really wanted God to love me so I read the Bible every day. That's how I thought I could learn the rules He expected me to abide by.

As I was learning God's rules, so was my mom. She taught us God's rules as well. Rules about obeying your parents. About not using the word hate because to hate someone was the same as committing murder. That we should do things without complaint when she told us what to do. She told us that we had to pray and read our Bible every day to make sure we stayed in God's good graces. She had many rules for us to follow and it was difficult to be perfect like she demanded.

Lucky for me, I continued to go to Kids of the Kingdom and learn about Jesus from Pastor Tim. He taught me about unconditional love and grace and peace. When I was in sixth grade, I earned a spot on the puppet ministry team, which also meant I was in a leader discipleship program. Once a week we had Bible study and puppet practice. My mom encouraged me to be involved because, according to her, the more work I did for God, the more He loved me.

Learning about God was extremely confusing. At church, from Pastor Tim, I learned that God loves everybody. That He offers grace to sinners. That we don't have to be perfect. That all of us have sinned and have fallen short of the glory of God. That God loves us so much that He sent His Only Son into the world to live and die so that we could be forgiven of our sins. I learned that God heals and offers peace and that when we pray and ask for things, God sometimes has to say no to keep us safe and in His will. I also learned that sometimes we make choices that aren't what God wants us to do, but He loves us anyway.

What I learned about God at church was not how my mom lived her Christianity or made us live ours. According to my mom you had to follow all the rules, perfectly, for God to love you. Rules like I could only be friends with other

Christians. Pray before eating. Protect your purity. Only date Christians. Don't swear or cuss. Don't listen to rock music. Don't listen to the radio. Stay away from ungodly things and people. Don't drink alcohol. Do what you're told. Don't smoke cigarettes or use drugs. If I did what I was supposed to do, God would love me and I'd go to heaven when I died. If I did what I wasn't supposed to do and I died, I'd go straight to hell.

At church, I learned about a loving God the Father and his Son Jesus, who died so I could be forgiven. At home, I learned about a harsh, judgmental God who couldn't wait to punish me for any wrong doing. I preferred the God that Pastor Tim was teaching me about to my mom's God. Unfortunately, when I was in eighth grade, Pastor Tim moved away and left our church. My mom decided that we would change churches too.

At our new church, I joined right in and got involved with the puppet ministry. I also started to attend youth group. Being involved in church was the only activity I was allowed to do. At this new church, everyone seemed to know the same God my mom knew. I started to believe what they believed. I had to earn God's love and when you already feel worthless that's a daunting task. It was overwhelming to realize that I would never be good enough for my parents, or for God, but I was determined to do my best. I wanted God and my parents to love and accept me and I'd work as hard as I needed to just to make that happen.

I often wondered why my parents couldn't love me unconditionally. Would I ever be good enough for them? No matter how incredibly hard I worked to be good enough, it was never enough for them. If I brought home an A- grade, I was called stupid idiot because it wasn't an A.

The idea my mom had that God only loved us when we are about His business, is what got me back to church the weekend following my staying out for half the night. We needed to be there so God would love us. She was also extremely worried about what people would think of her if she wasn't in church. I didn't care why we were going back; I was just glad to be going back to church so soon. I needed to see Jay again.

Chapter Four

After sitting with my mom in church for two weeks, the first Sunday she allowed me back in children's church leadership was great. I don't remember what we taught the children or what songs we sang, but I do know that Jay paid attention to me. He complemented my outfit and my hair. He kept an eye on me and smiled whenever I caught his eye. It was amazing to have somebody that liked me. I had felt worthless for so long; the attention gave me a glimmer of hope that I was worth enough for somebody to notice me and be there for me.

Knowing I meant so little to my parents, made it a big deal that Jay liked me. My feelings of worthlessness made me believe that nobody could ever like me, Jay changed that. He brought light to my dark world. I decided that Sunday morning that I would do whatever it took to keep Jay interested in me.

After church that day, Jay invited me to lunch. I quickly asked my mom's permission. "Ma, can I go to lunch with Jay?"

"Of course not! You know we go to Grandma's house after church. What kind of question is that? Besides, you can't date until your fifteen."

"I'll be fifteen in just a few weeks. Please. He can bring me to Grandma's when we're done. Please?"

"No."

I let out a frustrated sigh, "fine. Can Jay come to Grandma's with us?"

"We'll go, without him. You can ask Grandma and if she says yes you can call him and tell him how to get there."

"Thank you! Thank you! Thank you!" I was ecstatic that I would get to spend time with him.

As soon as we got to my Grandma's house I asked, "Grandma, can my boyfriend, Jay, come over this afternoon while we're here?"

"A boyfriend? Is he a nice guy? Will he like egg salad sandwiches for lunch?"

"He is very nice, Grandma. And who wouldn't like your egg salad for lunch?" We had egg salad many times with her after church. She made the best egg salad.

"Then go ahead and bring him." She said, smiling.

"Thank you, Grandma! Can I use your phone to call him?" Barely containing my enthusiasm.

"Go ahead."

I skipped to the phone, picked up the receiver and punched in Jay's phone number. It rang twice before it was answered.

"Hello."

"Hello. Is Jay there?"

"Yeah, hold on." Then I heard "Jay, that girl's on the phone."

"Hey, Mishell."

"Hi, Jay. My Grandma says you can come over. Hope you like egg salad sandwiches."

"Great. I'll borrow my brother's car. How do I get there?"

I gave him directions and we hung up. It was impossible for me to sit still while I waited for him to get there. I wandered around Grandma's apartment while my family ate their lunch. Since I was so anxious, I chose to wait for Jay and eat lunch with him.

A half hour passed before my ever-supportive mom piped up with, "I guess he's not coming. I guess you're not that special to him after all. I guess he didn't really want to spend the afternoon with you."

Just like that I went from excitement to anxiety. Just a few hurtful words and my thoughts changed from, "I can't wait until he gets here!" to, "what if he doesn't like me anymore?" I asked permission to go for a walk before I cried in front of my mom.

    I walked out the door of my Grandma's apartment in turmoil. One remark from my mother made me question whether or not Jay actually liked me. Maybe his brother wouldn't let him borrow the car. Maybe he got lost. He had been paying attention to me all morning during children's church. He had smiled at me and asked me to lunch. I worked hard to convince myself that my mom was wrong, that Jay did want to spend the afternoon with me and that something else was keeping him away.

    Walking down the parking lot of the apartment complex to the street, I looked up and smiled. Jay was walking towards me. He had changed out of church clothes and was dressed casually in a pair of shorts and a T-shirt. He was smiling too.

    "Sorry it took so long for me to get here," he began, with a hug. "Johnny wouldn't let me borrow the car until I went to get him lunch."

    Hugging him back with my cheek on his chest I replied, "It's alright. Ready to meet my Grandma and have lunch?"

    He laced his fingers through mine and we walked hand in hand back to my Grandma's apartment. My new world was right once again. Jay was here with me.

    We walked into my Grandma's apartment and I introduced him to her. She got up and made lunch for us. She was awesome like that. She always liked to make food for us. While she was making our lunch, Jay began a conversation with my mom.

    "I would really like to take Mishell on a date."

    "Well, she can't date until she's fifteen. Her birthday's in a few weeks. We can talk more about it then. She's starting tenth grade this year. What grade are you in?"

"I'll be a senior this year."

"What school do you attend?"

"Edison."

"My niece went there. She graduated in 1983, though, so you probably wouldn't know her." She laughed at herself. My mom often thought she was funny. She was not.

My Grandma came in with sandwiches for Jay and me. We ate, sitting at the table with her, my mom and my sister, Cindy. The conversation they were having before Jay arrived continued. He and I chimed in when we could, but it was difficult for me to follow the conversation with Jay sitting beside me. My mind was racing with thoughts about how he liked me. That he was here spending time with me, getting to know my family. How lucky I was to be Jay's girlfriend. I finally felt a little bit of worth.

After lunch, we snuggled on the loveseat, watching television; I tucked myself in under his arm as he placed it across my shoulder. I held his hand over my shoulder and he stretched his free hand across to hold my hand on his lap. We were so intertwined that it was difficult for me to tell where I ended and he began. It was extremely comfortable being that close to him. I finally had hope that I could be rescued from my life of worthlessness.

Chapter Five

I was ecstatic when my three-week summer finally ended. Because of a new school schedule, I started my sophomore year at the beginning of July. The beginning of school meant that I was no longer grounded for staying out half the night. It also meant that I could use the phone for twenty minutes each day and watch television again. However, the best part about school starting again was that I could be out of the house for seven glorious hours a day, Monday through Friday. I would have a break from my bickering parents and siblings.

I'd still have to help with breakfast and dinner and making sure everyone did their homework, but it was much easier on a school schedule than during the summer with nothing else to focus on except each other and our parents. I looked forward to the routine of school. I liked the structure and clear, obtainable expectations. I didn't get in trouble at school or draw attention to myself, I just did the work and got good grades.

School was a welcome change of scenery, but I was still isolated there with only a few friends. I did my best to not stand out, just do my work and get good grades so I wouldn't get in trouble at home. I had classes with people I had known for years at school, however, except for a couple of people, school was the extent of our relationship.

I ate lunch with a few friends on that first day of school. I told them about my new boyfriend, Jay, and how cute he was and how much he liked me. They didn't seem as excited as I was about having a boyfriend. My friends were more interested in their classes and teachers than they were in me and my life. Nobody cared that I had a boyfriend or that I had been grounded all summer. I was worthless at school too.

I spent time in my next class writing a letter to Jay, barely listening to my teachers, it didn't matter because it was all the same stuff on the first day of school. I daydreamed about Jay and how nice life would be once I could start going on dates with him. He'd take me to dinner and the movies, we could hang out together, at his house of course, away from my parents.

My smile never left my face. I was wanted by someone. Jay honestly wanted to be around me. He got involved in children's ministry at church just to be around me. After spending my life feeling dismissed and unimportant, it was nice to finally feel wanted.

That Wednesday was youth group and I got to see Jay again. My heart melted when I saw him. We went in to youth group, sat down together and worshipped God. I felt that God must truly be happy with me at that moment. I was doing my best to keep my parents happy. You know the fifth commandment, "Honor your father and mother so that your days might be long." (My paraphrase of course). Besides keeping my parents happy, I had a Christian boyfriend and read the Bible every day. I was doing what God wanted. Based on what my mom had taught me, I knew that God wanted me to date a Christian and not be "yoked to an unbeliever." It was good that my boyfriend was a Christian; it kept God and my mom satisfied.

If I did all the right things and said all the right things God would look down from heaven and make my life easier. I just wanted to be loved and valued, which was what Jay was giving me.

When my mom came to pick me up from youth group that night, Jay asked her if he could pick me up after school on my birthday and take me for a picnic. Surprisingly she said yes, as long as he had me home by five o'clock to do my homework and make dinner. It was a plan.

The next week and a half went by in a blur. I did everything my parents asked me to do to the best of my ability. I didn't want them to have any excuse to cancel my birthday date with Jay. That birthday was the first time I had ever had to be in school on my birthday, since I had a July birthday, and it sucked. Not one of my friends remembered it was my birthday. Oh well, my boyfriend was going to celebrate with me after school.

Jay was parked across the street from the busses after school. It seemed my feet never touched the ground as I walked to his car and slid in next to him on the bench seat. He drove us out to a county park near my house. Once he parked the car, we both slid out the driver's side door. We walked hand in hand to the trunk which Jay opened and pulled out a blanket and a bag of goodies. We found a shady spot beneath a large oak tree and spread out the blanket in the shade of its enormous canopy. I sat down and watched the sun dance through the leaves making shadows on the ground around Jay as he pulled the sandwiches and sodas out of the bag.

I felt so special that day and it was all because of Jay. I couldn't remember the last time I had celebrated my birthday, maybe when I turned nine. That was the year I received my first camera and I don't remember any birthday celebrations after that, not even with just my family.

Jay, on the other hand, had taken time out of his day to plan this. He had made sandwiches, bought sodas, and brought a blanket. He even planned exactly where he was going to take me. I felt bad though, because I would never be able to make him feel as special as he made me feel.

"Happy Birthday, Mishell!" He said with a smile, waving his arm over the amazing picnic spread.

I couldn't hide how happy I was, my smile lit up my whole face. "Thank you!"

He leaned across the blanket and gave me a quick kiss. "Anything for my girl."

I was completely relaxed as we talked, laughed and ate. I wasn't worried about what to say or do. I wasn't afraid of saying anything to make him mad. I realized that he must like me a lot to do all this for me. I was thrilled to be there with him on that picnic blanket in the shade of a large oak tree. My first date, on my fifteenth birthday, with this amazing guy who planned an incredible afternoon just for me.

When we finished eating Jay scooted closer to me on the blanket, wrapped his strong arms around me and began kissing me. I was glad that he hadn't put onions on our sandwiches. I enjoyed kissing him. His lips were soft and his mustache tickled. He kissed my ears and neck. While kissing me, Jay began to softly run his hands up and down my back. My stomach did flip-flops. He moved his hands away from my back and gently touched my arms, neck, and cheeks. Getting caught up in the moment, I caressed his back, arms and neck.

His hands were constantly moving and it felt good having his fingers move lightly over me. Relaxing and exciting me at the same time. I couldn't believe he was this into me. It was exciting to be kissing him and touching each other.

After some time, his hands strayed from my back and arms to my thighs. He tried to get his hand in the hem of my shorts. I shifted my legs so he wouldn't be able to touch anything. After a few more unsuccessful attempts of getting in the leg of my shorts, he brushed his hand over my chest, reaching for my cheek. I blew it off as inconsequential. He didn't mean to touch me there. It was just an accident. I made all kinds of excuses for him because I didn't want to be uncomfortable with Jay. I continued kissing him and keeping my hands on acceptable parts of his body.

He attempted to move his hand under my shirt. That was blatantly obvious. What do I do? I didn't want to make him mad. I didn't want to upset him and ruin an otherwise perfect afternoon. I casually pushed his hand down and laced my fingers with his to keep his hand away from my chest.

His other hand found the hem of my shirt and he tried to inch his way in again. I held that hand as well, to keep it from roaming uncomfortably around my body. I enjoyed when he touched my arms and back, but I wasn't ready for him to touch some of the private places of my body.

I wanted to save myself for marriage. That's what God and my parents demanded. I was confused. If he was a Christian, why was he trying to touch me in places he shouldn't? How could I tell him to stop without making him angry? I didn't want him to stop liking me.

"What's wrong?" he whispered in my ear. His warm breath cascading down my neck, exciting me "Don't you like me?"

"Yes, I like you. Can't you tell?"

"Then why are you stopping me?"

"I've never done anything like this before." I replied instead of telling him I was uncomfortable or that I wanted to stop.

"It's okay." Kiss. "Just relax." Kiss. "I won't hurt you." Kiss.

"Promise?"

"Promise." Kiss. "I never want to hurt you."

I relaxed and quit trying to control where his hands went. He kept them outside of my clothes, but I was uncomfortable with where his hands grazed, rested or rubbed. I just wanted someone to love me, so I let him.

I learned from my parents that if you wanted to be loved, sometimes you had to put up with being treated badly. So, if I had to sacrifice my comfort a little to make him happy, I would do that. If he needed to touch me, that would be okay. I could tell him no later. He did keep his hands outside of my clothes, what more could I ask for?

Magical afternoons can only last for so long. We cleaned up the blanket and he took me home on time. Neither of us wanted me to be grounded again. He dropped me off at the end of my driveway, gave me a quick kiss and hug goodbye and watched as I walked to the house.

My dad was on the sidewalk as I rounded the house towards the door. "Were you out screwing around?"

"No, I was on a picnic with Jay. Ma said I could." I reminded so he couldn't get mad.

"I know, she told me. Good thing you got home on time."

I didn't know how to respond, but I was thankful that was the end of the conversation. I wouldn't get in trouble because I was home on time. I continued past him into the house and started making dinner for the family before doing homework.

Sleep eluded me that night. I was completely confused. On one hand, I was happy. I had a boyfriend who cared enough to plan an incredible afternoon picnic to celebrate my fifteenth birthday with me. On the other hand, I had a boyfriend who didn't respect my body, by continuing to touch me after I told him I was uncomfortable. I guess I never told him I was uncomfortable though, only that I had never done that before. So, it was actually my fault that I was uncomfortable, but I was too afraid of upsetting him to say anything because I wanted him to like me. There was no way I would talk to my mom about it. She would make me break up with him and I didn't want to do that because I was finally special and that was something she would never understand.

A few days after my birthday date, my mom asked me to go outside with her while she smoked so we could talk. All the "important" talks happened while she smoked. I hated it! It was disgusting. I guess she did it for privacy because none of us wanted to be around her when she smoked, so she was guaranteed to have only the one she wanted with her.

"So, Mishell. You've been dating Jay for about a month now."

I nodded. Trying not to breathe as she exhaled a plume of smoke.

"I just want you to know that teenage boys only want one thing from teenage girls; sex."

I could feel the blush rising on my cheeks and I quickly looked away. I couldn't believe she was having this conversation with me. I wanted the ground to open up and swallow me whole. I wanted to be anywhere, but with my mom at that moment.

"You spent the other afternoon with Jay on your little date. Did he try anything? You know did he pressure you for sex?"

I emphatically shook my head, "no," still unable to speak. She already thought Jay only wanted sex. I would not tell her where he touched me while we were kissing. That would just confirm it in her mind, unless she already knew, but, how could she?

"If he hasn't yet, he will. It's all those teen-age boys want. You have to be strong though. You have to maintain your purity. You are the guard of your virginity. It's up to you to stop him from going all the way. Boys will be boys, you know."

"Okay." I mumbled. "Is that it? Can I go in now?" I wanted to crawl under a rock and never come out again.

She puffed on her cigarette and slowly blew the smoke in my direction. I gagged, gasping for fresh air.

"Yes, I'm done with you." She waved her hand in dismissal before continuing, "Just don't forget; you," she paused for emphasis, "are the guard of your purity."

I fled to the house like a thief fleeing the scene of the crime when the alarm sounds. I couldn't get away from her smoke or her little talk fast enough. I already let Jay touch more of my body than I was comfortable with. Granted it was all through my clothes so I was still a "good Christian girl." Or was I? Had I maintained my purity? I wanted to be a good Christian, but I wasn't sure if I still was. I knew I was not comfortable with where Jay's hands had been.

    I desperately wanted him to like me though. If I didn't let him touch me he might think that I didn't like him. Oh my God, I definitely liked him. I was one lucky girl to be with him. He celebrated my birthday for me, my own parents didn't so much as say happy birthday to me. I would have to tell him that his roaming hands made me uncomfortable.

    I hid in my room after that talk with my mom, contemplating what she had told me. All guys are only out for one thing. They all just want sex. If that's how they all were, what was the point of trying to keep one at bay or going so far as breaking up with him because where his hands ended up was bothersome to me? Wouldn't it be the same way with the next guy? And the one after that?

    I let Jay touch me where I shouldn't have. He didn't go beneath my clothes though, so maybe I was still a good girl. In the future, I would have to work hard to guard my purity and maintain my virginity.

Chapter Six

At school, a few days later, one of my friends invited me to her birthday party that Saturday. Of course, I asked if I could bring Jay along and she said yes. Now, all I had to do was get my parents to let me go. That was going to be easier said than done.

I went home after school, did my homework and got dinner ready. Whatever it took to have my mom in a good mood when I asked her if I could go to the birthday party.

When dinner was over and the dishes done, I mustered up the courage to ask her. "Ma, I have something to ask you."

"What do you want? I can tell by that voice you're using that you want something." She replied, irritated.

"Well, my friend, Rose is having a birthday party this weekend and she invited me." I kept my voice calm and sweet.

My mom sighed before continuing. "Will her parents be there?"

"Yes."

"Do you need me or your dad to drive you and pick you up?"

"That's the next part of my question. Can Jay take me? Rose said it's okay if he comes too." I rushed through before she could ask another question.

"Will he have you home on time?"

"Yes." Is what I said out loud. In my mind, I answered, of course he will, I don't want to be grounded from him ever again. He is my life.

"Will you only go to the party? Nowhere else? No parking on a dark country road to be alone? You know what he wants from you." Wagging her pointer finger in my face.

Exasperated with her questions, I contained my sigh. "We will only go to the party and come back home. What time will I have to be home?"

"Eleven o'clock. Not a second later."

"Yes, ma'am." I saluted her like she was a general. "Thank you!" I skipped to the phone and called Jay. I asked him if he'd like to go to the party with me and he said yes. I had my second official date with him planned. I couldn't wait!

I was even more excited when I could see Jay at youth group on Wednesday that week. My mom even allowed him to drive Stefyni and me. I was relieved that my sister was riding with us because I didn't want to have to tell him yet that his hands moving over my body made me uncomfortable. Having Stefyni in the car with us meant that conversation didn't have to happen just yet. The next time I would see him, we'd be at a party with other people there. I assumed he wouldn't have roaming hands in a crowd of people.

When Saturday came along, I woke up to help with breakfast. Then my brother, sister and I did all the Saturday chores; vacuuming, mopping, dusting, and cleaning the window sills and baseboards. Then I must have tried on every outfit I owned trying to find just the right thing to wear for the party. I attempted different hairstyles, straight, curled, up, down before I found the perfect hairdo; half up and straight as a board, my usual look. My outfit was shorts and a T-shirt. No matter how much I tried comfort always won out over fashion. When you feel like you don't matter, it doesn't matter what you look like either.

Jay picked me up right on time. I waited for him at the end of the driveway with my mom. We were outside, so of course she smoked. I stood as far away from her as I could to keep the cigarette stench from seeping into my hair and clothes. I hated that smell and I didn't want to take it to the party with me. I definitely didn't want Jay to smell it on me.

As soon as he pulled in the driveway I told my mom goodbye and walked to the passenger's side door. Jay reached across from the driver's seat and opened my door from the inside. It was sweet that he did that, it showed that he was a gentleman. When I was seated beside him, he gave me a quick kiss before he backed out.

He rested his hand on my thigh, just above the knee, while he drove with the other hand. One-handed driving made me nervous, but I wasn't going to say a thing. I enjoyed the casualness of his hand on my knee. It seemed as though we had known each other for months instead of weeks.

We pulled around the corner to Rose's house and the block was lined with cars. I didn't realize that many people would be at her party. The music could be heard when we got to her sidewalk. We walked to the door which was opened by her mom.

"Hey, you must be friends of Rose's. Welcome! Go on in, I'll be right back." She continued down the walk, climbed into the car in the driveway and drove away.

I grabbed Jay's hand as we walked inside. The music pounded in my ears, there were ice chests and people everywhere. Each person had a beer in hand.

"I had no idea it was this kind of party, Jay. I'm so sorry." I apologized in his ear to be heard above the music.

"It's fine. It's a party." He shrugged.

I had never been to a party with alcohol at it, so I was taken off guard. There were so many people there. Some of them were my age, but many seemed to be her parents' age.

Just then I saw my friend's dad, stumbling towards an ice chest. He was wearing nothing but a pair of well-worn boxers and had a beer in his hand. That didn't stop him from reaching in and grabbing another cold one. He staggered to where Jay and I were standing and asked me to hold the open can of beer while he popped the cold one.

I couldn't resist asking, "Why do you have two beers?"

"Well," he slurred. "Let me 'splain this to ya." His head bobbed up and down as he spoke as if his head was too heavy for his neck to hold up. "This beer," holding up the original can, "is warm. Warm beer's not good. So, I get a cold one," holding up the fresh beer, "but when I take a drink, it's too cold, so I drink the warm one to fix that. Then it's too warm so I drink the cold one." He held the cold one towards me before taking another swig. "Understand?"

Feeling it best to just agree, I nodded my head, "it makes perfect sense." Then he staggered to some other poor, unsuspecting guest and looked like he was explaining the same thing to them.

I wouldn't drink and Jay was driving, so we each grabbed a soda and went into the room where the music was coming from and started to dance, making sure not to spill our soda. At first the music was fast and fun with a good beat, then somebody put a slow, romantic song on. Jay took my soda from my hand and set them both on a table. He came back and put my arms around his neck then wrapped his arms around my waist, pulling me in, body to body, with him. He sang the song in my ears while we swayed to the music.

My soul was on fire. My heart was racing. My skin was tingling every place where our bodies touched. Feeling his breath on my neck as he sang in my ear sent chills down my spine. I just wanted to feel like that all the time. I didn't ever want to go home again and feel worthless. I wanted to stay in Jay's arms feeling wanted and special.

Jay refused to let go of me when the song ended. He held me in his arms and whispered in my ear, "I love you, Mishell."

I couldn't breathe. My thoughts were spinning. What did he just say? Did he just say that he loves me? What? This can't be real! This can't be happening! He loves me! God, Jay loves me! I pulled my head off his chest just enough to look in his deep, brown eyes and whispered, "I love you too, Jay."

I couldn't believe I had just said that to a boy. I thought nobody could ever love me. I was worthless, but maybe I wasn't. Maybe I had something to give. Maybe, my parents just couldn't see it. Maybe, just maybe, there was something to me.

It was a new thought, me being worth something, me having something to offer, me being good enough. I decided then and there, wrapped in Jay's arms that I would prove to Jay that I was good enough and that he wasn't wasting time with me.

He leaned down and kissed me soft on the lips. He pulled back still holding my hand and led me through the kitchen to the garage. Just inside the garage was a refrigerator off to the side. He leaned me up against it and started kissing me, gently at first but then intense, like he was starving for my affection.

I was thrilled. Parts of me that I didn't know could tingle, were tingling. I kissed him passionately. My hands roamed over his back, neck, through his hair. My back was to the refrigerator so he couldn't touch my back. He ran his fingers through my hair, traced my ears and down my neck. From there his hands continued down my chest, to the waistband of my shorts. I brushed his hands away, but continued to kiss him. He went right back to touching my chest, trying to slip his hand under my shirt.

Dammit, my mom was right. All boys want is sex. I can't keep this up. It's like he's an octopus with eight arms trying to touch me everywhere he shouldn't be. I can't keep brushing him off without upsetting him. I don't want to fight here. I don't t to fight at all. I just want to keep kissing and nothing more. Really, what's the point of fighting him off or telling him to stop if he's just going to keep trying?

I wasn't quick enough, he slipped his hand under my shirt and rubbed me through my bra. I couldn't breathe. I had failed. I wasn't able to keep my purity.

I kept kissing him. Why bother stopping him now? He had already touched me. I had already failed to keep his hands away. He kept moving his hand. He got a finger under my bra, on my skin. It felt like I had been burned. I wanted to cry, but I was too scared. Jay loved me. He just told me that. I didn't want to do anything that would jeopardize that so I let him continue.

Soon, his other hand was toying with my waist band. Then he slid it down my thigh to the hem of my shorts. He slipped his hand up my leg and touched me through my panties. I stiffened up and quit kissing him. He began to kiss my neck as his hand slid under my panties and he slipped his finger inside me. I gasped. He stopped. I asked him to take me home.

Chapter Seven

It was a silent awkward drive back to my house. All I could think about was that he had violated me and my trust. I was ashamed. It was my fault. I hadn't done enough to stop him. I should have talked to him about it before. I shouldn't have gone to the garage with him. I could have worn tighter shorts so he couldn't slide his hand inside. I wanted to crawl in bed and never come out. I wanted to take a shower to wash the filth away.

My mom was awake when I walked in the kitchen door, well before my curfew. "How was the party?"

"Fine. I'm going to take a shower and go to bed."

"What's wrong?"

"Nothing. I'm just tired." I lied.

I felt awful. I felt dirty. I was nauseous. My mind was racing. I was berating myself. I was angry. I was hurt. I was scared. I was worthless.

My mom was right. Boys only want one thing. I thought I made it clear by continually moving his hands that I didn't want him to touch me, but I didn't say no. Maybe he thought I was just being a tease. I wasn't strong enough to keep myself pure. I'm a terrible guard of my body. I'm no good at anything. I don't know if I can be his girlfriend because I don't want him to ever do that to me again.

I grabbed my pajamas off of my bunk and walked down the hall to the bathroom, silently scolding myself. I should have been stronger. I should have told him no. I turned on the water. I shouldn't have gone to the garage with him. I shouldn't have left the party. I climbed in the shower. I should have been more forceful in pushing his hand away. The warm water cascaded over me. The water mingled with my tears, flowing down the drain.

I still felt dirty. I turned the temperature up on the water hoping it would wash away the filth. I soaped up my washcloth and scrubbed all over, paying special attention to the places Jay had touched. I tried to wash away the memory of his violation of me. I made the water so hot it left red marks on my skin. The memory of his touch wouldn't go away. I couldn't wash it away no matter how hot the water was, or how hard I scrubbed.

I must be a horrible person. Jay said he loved me just a few minutes before he took me to the garage. If he loves me, why would he hurt me by doing something I was clearly not comfortable with? I wasn't firm enough or obvious enough. He must not have realized I was uncomfortable. I don't think he would hurt me on purpose, he loves me. I just won't be alone with him for a while. I don't want to make him angry and have him break up with me. I'll talk to him about it another time.

After the shower, I laid in bed for a long time. Replaying those moments in my head. Seeing it, feeling it, over and over. Each time the scene replayed I became more nauseous. I could tell my mom, but she would just tell me, "I told you so." I didn't want to hear that. I would have to make sure I wasn't alone with him again. Then he could never do that to me again.

The next day was his birthday. I had to see him at church. My plan was to act like nothing happened. If I just pretended it didn't happen, maybe it didn't. I was nervous to see him that morning. I didn't need to be, he acted as if he had done nothing wrong. No apology, no mention of the evening at all. That was alright by me. Ignoring the problem was the best way for it to be resolved. Right?

I got through church okay, but every time I thought about what I let Jay do to me, I got nauseous. I needed to go home. I needed to be away from him. We went to my Grandma's as usual. I didn't even ask if Jay could come with us. I didn't eat lunch with my family. While they ate, I laid curled up on the couch, with my knees to my chest, staring at whatever was playing on the television.

My mom looked at me from the table, "What is wrong with you, Mishell? You came home early last night and now you're not eating and you're just lying there like a bump on a log."

"I just don't feel good. My stomach hurts." It wasn't an out and out lie. I didn't feel good and I was nauseous. I could never tell her why though. She would have all sorts of wonderful names to call me if she knew that I let Jay touch me. She would call me a failure, a lousy guard of my body, a slut, a whore.

I called Jay when I got home later.

"How was your birthday?" I started.

"Alright."

Awkward silence. I was only allowed twenty minutes to use the phone and the minutes were slowly ticking away.

"How was your afternoon at your Grandma's?"

"Fine."

"About last night. I didn't mean to startle you."

"I was surprised and I'm not ready for that. I want to wait until I'm married to have sex." There. I said it. I was shaking, my hands were sweating. I would find out if I was still his girlfriend. I didn't want to be alone again.

"It's fine. Next time I won't surprise you like that."

"Thank you. I appreciate it." He didn't break up with me. My heart soared.

"Why don't you want to have sex before you're married?"

"It's what the Bible says and I'm just not ready. Besides my parents would kill me if they ever found out." Having told him I didn't want to have sex, and him not breaking up with me or getting mad gave me courage and broke my nervousness.

"Why would your parents find out? You plan on telling them when you have sex?"

"Uh, no." I sarcastically answered.

"Besides what we did wasn't actually sex. It was just fooling around. I don't think the Bible has anything to say about that. Does it?"

I paused, "I guess not. It talks about fornication though, which is sex outside of marriage."

"Like I said, that wasn't sex. That was just messing around. I think God is okay with that."

I didn't argue. I knew I couldn't win. I never won arguments and I didn't want to win this one at the cost of losing Jay. The situation just made me feel worse about myself.

Being Jay's girlfriend allowed me a sense of freedom from my parents that I didn't have before. Even though I stayed out half the night when I met him, they were allowing me more freedom. My parents would never have let me go to Rose's party if they would have had to drive me. The last party my parents drove me to, I was in eighth grade.

A friend of mine had a birthday party on a weekend. It was the first boy-girl party I had been invited to and I was super excited to go. I got there early, a bad habit of mine, and got to greet people as they arrived. A lot of students from my classes were there. We danced, talked, laughed and generally had fun.

My dad was supposed to pick me up at ten o'clock so at 9:55 I checked out the window because I didn't want to wait outside alone. He wasn't there yet so I danced a little more. I checked again a few minutes later. He still wasn't there. I listened to someone tell a joke. Peeked outside again, still no dad. I kept checking every few minutes and he never showed up.

At 10:15 or so, I asked to use the phone. I called my house. My dad answered the phone after four rings.

"Speak."

"When are you coming to get me?"

"I already did. You weren't there. I came home."

"I checked. I didn't see you." I explained.

"You should've been outside waiting for me when I got there. You weren't waiting and neither was I."

"Are you going to come back and get me?" Thinking that he wouldn't just leave me there.

"Nope."

"How am I supposed to get home?"

"Walk for all I care, but you better get your stupid ass home." Click. He hung up on me.

I cried. He left me at a party a ten-minute car ride from home. He expected me to get a ride on my own. I was in eighth grade, so we're my friends. We didn't drive. I don't remember how I got home, but I did somehow and my parents have refused to drive me to a party since.

The fact that my parents were allowing Jay to drive my sister and me to youth group now and letting me go out with him one night each weekend was a real win for me. I didn't want to lose that extra time away from home. I thought I would lose that freedom if I pushed Jay to stop touching me because I thought he'd break up with me. If remaining his girlfriend meant that I had to give up a part of my body, then that's just the way it would be. How I felt didn't matter as much as the fact that somebody loved me.

Chapter Eight

Since I had been dating Jay, my dad distanced himself even more from me and my mom acted like she finally liked me. My dad was there just enough to disregard my feelings for Jay and to let me know that he knew I was screwing around with every Tom, Dick and Harry. (One of his favorite lines to me.) My mom was there teaching me to always be on guard when I was with Jay, but allowing me more and more time alone with him. It seemed like a contradiction to me. On one side, she was telling me that he only wanted to have sex with me, that's what all guys wanted, and on the other she was allowing me to be alone with him. It was terribly confusing.

By the time that Jay and I had been dating for about six months, it was a given that he would join us at my Grandma's or Cindy's house on Sunday afternoon. I was also allowed to go on dates with him one weekend night and I could hang out with him on Saturdays. It was a big change for me. For most of my life, I hadn't been allowed to hang out with people outside of our family or church. I had been to a few sleepovers in junior high and elementary school, but they were few and far between.

I was getting to see how other people lived and behaved outside of my family on a regular basis. Granted, it was only one other family, but it was still different from my own experience. The kids had freedom, they didn't always have to get permission to go somewhere, and they didn't even always tell their mom where they were going, with whom and when. That was unheard of in my family.

For my dad to give approval for any plans I had to ask permission at least twenty-four hours in advance or else the answer would be "NO!" I mean, twenty-three hours and fifty-nine minutes was too close to when the plan was happening to get a positive answer. Then when I asked permission, I had to be able to answer all the questions about who, what, when, where, and how. If I couldn't answer all the questions, then I didn't get to participate in the activity.

My mom was a bit more lenient on letting me do things, especially if it was with Jay. I could start a sentence with, "I think Daddy would say no, but…" and as long as somebody else was driving me and it involved Jay or someone from church she usually would allow me to participate. Needless to say, Jay ended up driving me to lots of activities besides the dates we went on.

Even though Jay and I had been dating for six months by then, I was still uncomfortable with what he wanted to do when we were alone. He always wanted to put his hands inside my clothes and touch me in places I didn't want to be touched. After months of fighting him off, I just accepted the fact that it was going to be that way if I was going to continue dating him. I wasn't going to break up with him over it. He liked me, I liked him, I liked that he liked me and my mom seemed to like me since I started dating him.

On one Sunday afternoon at my sister's house, my mom sent Jay and I to the store. I was happy to go because it meant time away from my mom and annoying little brother. It also meant she trusted me and was giving me responsibility. However, I was also anxious about going because it meant that I would be alone with Jay.

"Come on Mitch. Let's go." He proposed. I cringed.

I got the money from my mom and walked out the door to the car. He followed me and got in the driver's seat as I climbed in the passenger side without saying a word.

"What's wrong, Mitch?"

"I don't like when you call me that." I replied.

"Why not, Mitch? Cindy calls you that and you don't seem to mind."

"I don't mind when she calls me that, but I don't like it when you do." I explained with clenched teeth.

"Why not?" he questioned me.

"It makes me feel like you think I'm a boy." My shoulders slumped as I admitted this to him.

I hated to admit that to him, but I was self-conscious about it, with all people, not just Jay. I didn't dress frilly and girly, I didn't wear makeup, and most days I did nothing with my hair, except brush it. I preferred jeans and a T-shirt, no makeup and hair half up in a clip. I always favored comfort over fashion and it had made me a target of teasing when I was younger. I still worried about it. When my sister called me Mitch, it was just what she called me, I didn't care, but it really bothered me when Jay did it.

"Now that you mention it, you could use some makeup. Maybe a dress every once in a while. You know, look like a girl, Mitch"

My heart sank. A lone tear slipped from my eye and trailed down my cheek before I wiped it away. How could he say that to me? For the past six months, I was good enough for him and now I'm not. I thought he liked me for me. Especially after all I had let him do to me. Every time we were alone all he wanted to do was get his hands in my pants. My clothes only seemed to be in his way, I didn't think it mattered what they looked like to him. I stared out the window as we drove to the store, wondering what I should do. He parked near the store, turned off the car, turned to face me and placed his hand on my knee.

"Look, Mitch, I love you. It doesn't matter that you look like a boy to me. But it might to other people. You're lucky I don't care about that because nobody else would be as nice about it as me. You're lucky to have me. I'm sorry I made you feel bad."

I turned to face him, clearing all emotion from my face. He was smiling at me. The hurt and anger washed away when I looked into his sweet and honest eyes. I was lucky to have him. He loved me with all my insecurities, my crazy family and their insane rules. Growing up in my family taught me that when somebody loves you, you put up with a lot of bad stuff waiting for the moments that mean something, no matter how fleeting or rare those good moments were.

I had a couple of good memories that I clung to, hoping my parents would show me affection. When I was about five years old, I had gone out with my dad to feed the calves. On our way back to the house, he came up behind me, scooped me up in his arms and swung me into a big hug. This memory of my dad's love and protection carried me through the difficult times with him.

The other memory I held on to was that when I was a little girl, my mom was a nurse and worked until almost midnight. Many nights when she came home, I would be awake waiting for her. She would let me have a Popsicle and snuggle on the couch with her until I finished eating it. Then she would tuck me into bed and tell me she loved me. Those fleeting memories gave me hope that my mom could truly love and accept me.

I knew that the same thing was happening with Jay. He may have hurt my feelings, he may have violated my body, but he loved me so I put up with the bad waiting for the good. It wasn't ideal, but it was the best a girl like me could hope for.

Jay leaned over and kissed me on the cheek before getting out of the car. We walked in to the store hand in hand. He was back. He loved me again. We walked through the store filling the cart with items from my mom's list, talking like nothing had happened. We checked out and loaded up the car. He opened my door for me, making me feel significant. Everything was forgiven.

I didn't recognize the way he was driving to get back to my sister's house. I quickly realized that he was taking me to a deserted place to park, but I was used to that now. He pretty much made sure that we had a make out session, at some point, every time we were alone together and his hands never stayed in safe places. I didn't even fight him anymore, I just let it happen.

He parked the car off the road with no houses to be seen and only open fields, dotted with cows, as far as I could see. As soon as the car was in park he put his hand behind my neck and pulled me into a deep kiss. His hands moved under my shirt and unbuttoned my jeans. Then he stopped.

I looked at him in shock; thankful that he stopped.

Then he grabbed my hand.

"Let me show you what I like." He unzipped his pants, pulled his underwear down and put my hand on him.

His hands went back to what he was doing to me while he kissed me and whispered instructions in my ear. When he was done, he stopped touching me, stopped kissing me, adjusted himself back into his underwear, zipped up his pants and drove us back to my sister's house with my mom's groceries.

I was horrified. I had never experienced that. I had to clean my hand. I found a napkin in the glove box. It disgusted me. I felt so dirty and used. He acted like it was no big deal. He didn't say a word as we drove. When we got to my family he acted completely normal with them, as if nothing had just happened. As though he hadn't just made me do something I never wanted to do.

All I wanted to do was to go home. I was nauseous. I felt worse than I did the first time he had violated me at Rose's party. I wanted to take a shower and wash the reminder of him off my hand.

While he helped my family put the groceries away, I went directly to the bathroom, turned the water in the sink to full hot and pumped soap into my hands. I placed my hands under the water, adjusted it to as hot as I could handle and scrubbed my hands as hard as I could. I wanted to get Jay off my hand. The memory of what he made me do needed to wash down the drain like the soap and water that were swirling away.

That would be an expected part of being alone with him now, and I didn't like the idea, but what could I do? If I broke up with him, my mom would want to know why and I was too mortified to tell her. I didn't want to hear what she would have to say to me; the names she would call me. Besides, I really enjoyed the freedom and the relative ease of our relationship for the past six months or so that I had been dating Jay. She seemed easier to get along with since Jay and I would go do things for her. She even used the fact that he was eighteen years old to her advantage by having him buy cigarettes for her.

I scrubbed my hands until the hot water ran out. I dried them, still trying to wipe the memory away and dreading going out to the living room with everyone else. I was afraid my face would give away my disgust with Jay and myself. I used the mirror to practice wiping all emotion from my face. Attempting to disguise my true feelings as happiness and contentment. When I had mastered the mask, I joined my family and Jay in the living room, watching movies.

I sat near Jay, but not right next to him. He noticed and scooted so close our bodies were touching. A new wave of shame swept over me, but I held my composure. I had to hide my feelings to keep anyone from knowing how embarrassed and ashamed I was for what I allowed Jay to make me do to him. I had been able to get over what he liked to do to me; I would have to get over this too. He draped his arm casually over my shoulder as we watched the movie with my family. It took everything in me to not visibly cringe when he touched me.

I convinced myself that everything was okay. I told myself that I was just being too sensitive about him calling me

Mitch. I scolded myself for feeling bad about what we did. It wasn't like it was real sex, it was just messing around. I didn't need to feel ashamed, or guilty or anything. It was something that happened. That's it.

But that wasn't it.

Chapter Nine

My family got shocking news in April of that year, just a few months after that horrendous Sunday afternoon with Jay. My cousin, who was a few years older than me, was getting married because he got his girlfriend pregnant. It shocked us because he was a "good Christian boy." He wasn't supposed to be having sex with his girlfriend and if he did, she sure as heck wasn't supposed to get pregnant. The whole family, aunts, uncles and cousins were invited to the wedding on May 5th.

As surprised as I was that my cousin was getting married and becoming a dad, I was excited for the wedding because my old children's Pastor, Tim, would be officiating the ceremony. I hadn't seen him since I graduated from eighth grade, almost two years earlier. I had only talked to him a few times. I really missed Pastor Tim and the way that he taught me about who Jesus was. I couldn't wait for my cousin's wedding!

Wedding Day finally arrived. I sat anxiously in the backseat as my mom drove through town looking for the hall where the ceremony would take place. As soon as we parked I jumped out of the car so I could see Pastor Tim. I ran up to him and gave him the biggest hug I could. I felt all my shame and guilt wash away when he hugged me back. For a moment, I felt as if I was good enough for God. My body relaxed and my thoughts stopped racing. It was a peaceful moment in my otherwise chaotic life.

My family came and dragged me away from Tim so that he could prepare for the ceremony. My mom led my siblings and me to a row near the front of the hall. We sat and waited. And waited. And waited. His fiancé was there, waiting in the back of the room with her father to walk her down the aisle. She looked quite irritated that she was being kept waiting by my cousin.

There was a raucous outside that caused us all to look to the side door of the hall. My cousin and his friends were out there laughing, hollering and stumbling towards the building. My cousin tripped through the door and to the front of the hall near Pastor Tim.

My mom leaned over to my older sister and whispered, not so quietly, "Oh my God, he's drunk!"

He shouldn't have been drunk. He was a good Christian boy. I looked up to him as a role model. He let me down. Not only did he have sex and get his girlfriend pregnant, he drank too. He showed up drunk to his wedding. If he couldn't be good enough, how was I supposed to be good enough?

My mom was judging him for being drunk. She had been talking bad about him for the past few weeks for getting a girl pregnant. She continuously reminded me that all boys, even the good ones, only want sex. There was no way that I could tell her about what Jay and I did when we were alone, even though I still cringed whenever he wanted me to do it to him. It was a nice day without him.

If I broke up with him, my mom would judge me for leading him on for so long and then breaking his heart. Also, I liked the direction my relationship was going with her; we got along so much better since I started dating Jay. My dad would probably love it if I broke up with Jay. Our relationship was pretty much non-existent since I had been dating Jay. All he did now was yell at me and fight more often with my mom. A lot of their fights were about what my mom allowed, Stefyni and I to do and who we were with, especially Jay.

I was devastated as I watched my cousin get married. Everything that I thought was true in the world and my family was falling apart. I knew that my mom often said one thing and did another, but I never thought my cousin would. Tears filled my eyes and threatened to glide down my face. I blinked them away before anybody could see. I was heartbroken and empty. There was no point in continuing to try to live good enough for God or my parents. It was all so futile.

When the ceremony was over, I went to speak with Pastor Tim. He told me he had to leave because he had to get home to his family, but he wanted to talk to me for a second.

"I hear you have a boyfriend, Mishell."

I smiled, "I do." How did he know?

"Is it Jay?"

"Yes." My eyes grew large as saucers. Pastor Tim even knew who it was.

"You know I only want the best for you, Mishell. I think you need to be careful with him."

"I am." It seemed like he knew what Jay did to me and what Jay made me do to him. Guilt and shame enveloped me. I still felt empty. It was the first time being around Pastor Tim that I felt like nobody could reach me.

"I mean extremely careful, Mishell. Understand?"

"Yes, I do. I'll be careful." I heard the words come from me, but there was no emotion connected to them.

"Be good, Kiddo. Love you." He hugged me.

"Love you, too." The words sounded hollow in my own ears. The words were true, Pastor Tim was one of the most influential people in my life, but at that moment, I had no love to give.

With that Pastor Tim said his goodbyes to the rest of the family and drove away.

Driving home with my mom was miserable. It was a non-stop rant about my cousin and all the bad decisions he had been making. She went on to how mortified she would be if one of her kids made these types of embarrassing choices.

She wouldn't want people to think she was a bad mother with children who disobeyed her.

I was empty. I had nothing left inside. I couldn't muster up even a miniscule amount of emotion to care about anything. I couldn't even be angry at my mom for how judgmental she was being towards by cousin and my aunt. I was a worthless, used, broken shell. I truly was lucky that Jay loved me, because I didn't think anybody else could.

The day after my cousin's wedding was Sunday. I went to church as usual. I helped in children's church and performed a song with the puppets. It was a typical Sunday for me, except I was wearing a skirt instead of my usual jeans and a blouse. Jay's comments a few months earlier had made me even more self-conscious than I already was about how I dressed, so I bought a skirt.

The denim skirt and white blouse with the silver buttons looked nice on me. It was still denim, which was comfortable for me, but to make Jay happy I was wearing a skirt. I looked like a girl, but I felt like a sellout, just to keep Jay interested. He was becoming more demeaning of me about how I looked and acted, and I didn't even care. If nobody else really loved me, why should I?

All through church I couldn't help but wonder why Pastor Tim had told me to be careful with Jay. It seemed like he knew something I didn't. Every time I looked at Jay, I wondered what it could be that Pastor Tim was warning me about.

After church, my mom allowed me to spend the afternoon with Jay and I was glad to have the opportunity to be away from my family. I assumed we'd hang out at his house or with a friend. At lunch, he told me a friend asked us to get something from their apartment for them. Whatever. I didn't care.

When we got to the apartment complex, he parked and we walked together to the apartment. I was a little uneasy, I thought about what Pastor Tim had said the day before, but I brushed the feeling aside. I was excellent at pushing my feelings aside to keep others happy with me.

Jay held my hand and led me into the apartment. We sat down and he started kissing me. He nibbled my ears and kissed down my neck. I mentally prepared myself for what I thought would be next. What he had been making me do to him since that afternoon in the car on the way back to my sister's house.

"I love you, Mishell. You know that, right?" he whispered in my ear.

I nodded. "I love you too."

"Good, because I want more. I'm done with just messing around. It's time you stop teasing me." He whispered in my ear while he laid me down with his arm across my chest, pinning me.

I couldn't catch my breath.

With his other arm, he took his own pants down.

My heart raced.

He reached under my skirt.

My mind was spinning.

He moved my panties aside.

Chills washed over me.

He forced himself inside of me.

I wriggled against the cushions, trying to get away, but he was twice my size. He pressed his arm tighter across my chest. I was a scrawny little girl compared to him.

He told me to relax; that I'd enjoy it. I couldn't relax and I didn't enjoy it.

It hurt.

I cried.

He finished, told me to stop crying and to go clean up so we could leave.

My legs shook as I walked to the bathroom. The reality that I was no longer a virgin hit me like a ton of bricks and I collapsed against the wall before standing up again. I thought I was empty the day before at my cousin's wedding when I realized being good was futile, now I was truly, completely empty. I was a broken, hollow shell of a person. There was no point in fighting him anymore. Nobody else would ever want to be with me because I was used goods. My virginity was gone. I didn't have that special part of me to offer anyone again.

For ten and a half months I had been able to avoid having sex with him. In one afternoon, in less than five minutes, the fight was over. Nothing mattered anymore. I was used up, unimportant. I was completely worthless.

That day my life went from bad to worse. I had never felt good enough for God, parents, teachers, or friends, but I always tried. I had wanted so badly to be loved and accepted. Not anymore. I would never be good enough, I wasn't even good.

I quit trying to win my parents' approval. I stopped caring about whether or not God loved me. I didn't even care if Jay loved me. I was too embarrassed to break up with him, because my mom would want to know why. I couldn't tell her that I had sex with him. It would mean that she was right all along. I even gave up in school. I did just enough to keep from being noticed.

I gave up.

Chapter Ten

I was empty and withdrawn. At home, I did my best not to interact with my family. I did what was expected of me and slept a lot. My dad yelled at me more than he used to, but his tantrums couldn't reach me. He couldn't make me feel any worse than I already did.

I continued to see Jay, because that's what was expected of me. My mom thought he was a great guy. He helped in the children's church and he was very respectful to her. She had no idea that every time he and I were alone together he forced me to have sex with him.

Each time it happened I called myself a slut and whore. Jay didn't help at all by telling me that's what people would call me if they ever found out, especially my mom. Eventually, it didn't even phase me anymore. There was no way I could feel anymore empty or worthless.

Sophomore year ended and like the summer before I was stuck at home. My mom worked, my dad didn't, but he was rarely home, that left me in charge of Stefyni and Keeth. One bright spot in the two-month summer at home was that just like the previous summer my youth group planned extra activities. One of the events that I was especially looking forward to was a day at an Oakland A's baseball game. I had never been to a professional game of any sport and was extremely excited about the experience.

The day of the game arrived. In our excitement and rush to go, Stefyni and I both completely forgot to do the breakfast dishes before we left. That one slip up would have a devastating impact on our lives. At least we had the day at the game.

We got home after dark, but not too late for curfew. Walking up the driveway, I noticed a pile of stuff outside our bedroom window. I couldn't make out what it was in the dark, but figured that my dad had been busy with something. There were always stacks and piles of junk that he moved around the property.

We used the door nearest our bedroom to enter the house into the kitchen. The floor was littered with broken bits and pieces of bowls and plates. There was silverware everywhere. The dishwasher door was open and the shelves inside were empty. Before we had the door shut, my dad was hollering at us from his spot on the living room couch.

"Where the hell have you two shit-for-brains been all God damn day?"

"At the baseball game." I stammered.

"Who the hell gave you permission to go without doing the God damn dishes?"

"Ma, said we could go." My hands shook as much as my voice.

"Without doing the dishes? You know you're not allowed to go anywhere without getting your chores done first."

"Sorry. We forgot." I tried.

"You didn't forget; you chose not to do them. You don't forget! You probably didn't even go to the game; you were probably out fucking Jay and Dustin. Clean up the mess in the kitchen!"

It took about an hour to clean up all the dishes. We started with the silverware and the plates and bowls that didn't break. Then we dug the vacuum out of the closet to get all the tiny pieces. When we were done cleaning up the floor, he made us wash the dishes that hadn't been shattered.

Another surprise awaited us when we were finally allowed to go in our bedroom. The window was open, the screen gone and everything was in a pile outside the window. The pile I had seen walking up the driveway.

When I say everything, I mean everything. My bedroom had been thrown out the window. The only items remaining in our room were the dresser frame, the bunk bed frame and the desk. Our clothes, papers, mattresses, stuffed animals, bedding, hangers, dresser drawers; absolutely everything was in a pile outside of our window. We were stunned.

I was standing in the center of my empty room, beside Stefyni, staring at all my stuff in the pile outside, when my dad came into the room and threw two phonebooks at us.

"I have a phone number. I want you two shit-for-brains to figure out who it belongs to." He handed us a scrap of paper with a phone number on it. "If you don't figure it out, I'll have a bonfire in the morning with all your stuff out there."

Stefyni and I slumped down to the floor and each picked up a phone book. I started with the first page reading phone numbers instead of names. When I finally reached the end of the phone book without finding the number it was the wee hours of the morning. My eyes ached and I could barely keep them open.

I closed the phone book and finally spoke, "Did you find it, Stef?"

"No. Did you?"

"Nope. What do we do now? Go tell your dad that we couldn't figure it out and wait for him to burn our stuff?" That's not what I wanted to do

"I say we go to sleep and wait for him to come in." Stefyni suggested with a yawn.

"That's sounds good to me. I hope he doesn't really burn our stuff." I offered.

"Me too." She responded before curling up on the floor.

We slept for a few hours before our dad came in to our room, waking us up with, "Did you figure it out?"

It was still dark outside when I opened my eyes. I looked up at my dad from the floor and shook my head, "No. We didn't find it. Are you going to burn our stuff now?" I grumbled.

He laughed. "I didn't expect you to find the fucking number. I just made it up and wanted to know if it belonged to somebody. Go start breakfast. After you eat you can get your shit put away."

That was it. He acted like he didn't just empty the cabinets onto the kitchen floor, throw our bedroom out the window or threaten to burn all our stuff. I couldn't believe it. It was difficult to live in the same house with him. I walked on eggshells around him. It was getting worse and worse all the time. He and my mom had pretty much quit talking to one another. He only spoke to us kids to belittle us or tell us to do something. I was constantly afraid of what would happen next.

Later that day, he left and I was able to relax a bit. I began thinking about a way to break up with Jay without having to tell my mom why. I didn't want her to think I was a slut. My dad already thought I was a slut and he didn't even know that I let Jay have sex with me. I was tired of feeling empty and sad all the time. There were times that I had fun, like the baseball game, but the sadness and emptiness never went away. They were always there, holding onto me, keeping me down. Maybe if I broke up with Jay, I would start to feel better.

My sister, Cindy, happened to call that day after my dad left. She asked how things were going. I told her what my dad had done the night before; throwing all of our stuff out the window, breaking all the dishes and threatening to burn all of our stuff. She was as shocked as we had been when we saw it the night before. She felt bad for us and said she'd try to do something to help us.

I had no idea what she meant, but it didn't take long to find out.

Chapter Eleven

About a week after the room dumping event, my mom received a phone call that informed her that if she didn't remove the three of us kids from the house where my dad lived, we would be removed to the county children's home. She agreed to move us out of my dad's house to keep us from the county shelter, but she had to make plan.

The children's director from our church met with us at a local pizza place to devise a plan. Dustin and Jay met us there too. My mom needed money to pay for the deposit and first month's rent in order to move. Unfortunately, she didn't have any money saved and we needed to move by the end of the next week.

I sat and listened like an audience member in a play as they talked things out. They decided that Stefyni, Keeth, my mom and I would move into Jay's house, with his family, until my mom saved enough money for our own place. She figured it would take about two weeks. They also came up with a way for us to move out of my dad's house without him knowing and trying to stop us.

The day after the pizza parlor planning session was the first day of my junior year of high school. What a way to be starting the year; homeless. We went to school that day, but according to the plan, on the second day of school we walked to the end of the driveway where we usually caught the bus, but instead of getting on the bus Dustin and Jay picked us up and took us to Jay's house.

When my dad left the house, we drove back there with two cars and a pick-up. We worked together to quickly pack our things and loaded it all into one of the cars or the truck. It took about an hour to get all of our stuff packed and loaded. We didn't have much.

It didn't take long to unload everything and before too long we had our dressers set up in Jay's garage and our pillows and a few other things with us inside the house. Stef, Keeth, my mom and I were sharing Jay and his brother's room. They would sleep on the couch. I laid down when we were done unloading and it dawned on me that I was homeless. Jay's family had given us a place to stay for a few weeks, but really I had no home. I grew up constantly going back and forth between my mom's house and my dad's house and never felt at home at either. Now I had no family home to go to at all.

I went back to school the next day still trying to wrap my head around the fact that I was homeless. I also tried to keep it to myself which was pretty easy to do since I didn't have too many friends at school; especially since I had started dating Jay. The only friend who I still had regular contact with was Shauna, but we didn't have any classes together that year.

My worthlessness was the only thing I could focus on all day. Nobody spoke to me all day, like I wasn't even there. None of my teachers even asked why I had been absent the day before. It magnified my worthlessness and proved I was invisible. It was obvious, nobody cared about me.

Jay picked me up from school that day and took Stefyni and I back to his house. He immediately took me to his sister's room where we could be alone. He didn't ask how my day had been, or how I was feeling with all the crap going on in my life. No, he just started kissing me, taking my clothes off and doing what he wanted to me. It didn't matter to him that my mom was in the next room. When I reminded him of that fact, he just told me to be quiet so she wouldn't be able to hear anything.

Two weeks after moving out of my dad's house we moved out of Jay's house into a place of our own. I was grateful that we hadn't had to live in the car, but every day of those two weeks, Jay made sure that we had time alone so that he could do what he wanted with me. There was no way that I could break up with him after he and his family let my entire family stay with them when we needed to leave my dad's house and had nowhere else to go.

I had a lot more freedom living with my mom than I was used to having when we lived with my dad. My mom's health became worse; she was unable to work much and spent time in the hospital. Because of her ill health, she basically allowed me to go where I wanted, when I wanted, if I was home by curfew. Just a year before, that would have been incredible for me. I would have appreciated the freedom, but now it meant that I had to spend more time with Jay. My mom thought the sun rose and set with him after how helpful he was to us, so I wouldn't tell her what he was really an animal who couldn't keep his paws off of me.

Not too long after we moved out of my dad's house, Iraq invaded Kuwait. The next day at school, all my teachers did was either watch the news to see what was going on, or talk about the United States going to war with Iraq. The world was as hopeless as I was. Nothing was going right in the world or my life.

When I walked in the front door of my house after school that day, Jay and Dustin were sitting on my couch with my mom, waiting for Stefyni and me to get home.

"We need to talk." Jay stated as soon as we walked in.

"All of us?" I asked more than a little confused.

"Well, Dustin's in it too." Jay answered.

"In what, exactly?" Stefyni questioned.

"We're going to join the Marines." Jay announced rather proudly.

"The Marines. Why?" I asked.

"Because the United States is going to war and I want to be in it." Jay explained.

"Exactly." Dustin agreed.

"Did you already sign up?" I was upset that he would make this kind of decision without talking to me, but not surprised.

"Not yet. We're going tomorrow." Dustin said.

"Nothing I can say will change your mind, Jay?" I asked because I thought that's what he wanted to hear.

"Nope! I want to do this."

"Whatever." I shrugged my shoulders. "I have to do homework." I was trying to look upset, but inside I was secretly happy. This could be the answer I was looking for.

I went to the dining table to do homework with Stefyni, while Jay and Dustin sat and talked to my mom about joining the Marines.

I wondered when he would leave for basic training because then I would be free of him. He'd be gone and I could safely break up with him and nobody would have to know the real reason why. It could be perfect. I hoped it would be soon. I never thought it was possible to feel as lonely as I did, especially being surrounded by people who were supposed to love me.

I hated my life so much that I began to think everything would be better if I could start over somewhere else. Meet new people, be away from my family and away from Jay. I fantasized about leaving, about running away. I didn't want to live my life any longer.

Everything sucked!

Unfortunately, there was no way for me to run away and start over right then. I didn't have a job, so I had no money. I was just a junior in high school and had no real skills. School would be the way to get myself out of the hole I was in. My grades hadn't gotten too low, I still had mostly B grades, but I started to apply myself more. It helped in all my classes except math and chemistry. I had not taken it seriously enough in the beginning and was pretty far behind in my understanding. I ended up having to drop chemistry at the semester and barely earned a D in math.

My mom's health continued to deteriorate. The doctors had no idea what was going on with her health, so they just kept treating symptoms and never finding the cause of her illness. She was unable to work or drive anymore. Because she couldn't drive, she suddenly became encouraging when I drove and was in a hurry for me to get my driver's license. I got my license in December of my junior year. That gave me the freedom to get a job so I could start saving my money for my new life. I filled out application after application and eventually got hired at an ice cream shop.

Having a job helped me feel better about myself and my life. I opened a bank account so I could start saving money. That would help me escape my current life and make it easier because I would be able to buy things I needed without having to rely on my mom. Having a job also meant that I had less time to spend with Jay. It was easy to stay away from him and what he did to me. I requested to be scheduled as many hours as my work permit would allow.

Because I worked more and saw Jay less, he would often hang out with me whenever he could. Even if it was only fifteen minutes while I was getting ready for work. On one of those days, he watched as I got ready for work. He even followed me into the bathroom as I put my hair up and brushed my teeth.

"What are you doing your hair for?" He demanded.

"I have to have it in a ponytail to keep it out of the ice cream." I explained.

"Why are you brushing your teeth? Who are you planning on kissing? That guy who works there?" His jealousy was showing.

"I don't plan on kissing anybody. I'm brushing my teeth because I want clean teeth and fresh breath when I help the customers." Rolling my eyes.

"That better be the case. If I ever find out, you cheated on me…" he raised his hand like he was going to backhand me. "You'll get this and so will the guy."

"I wouldn't cheat on you. You know that." I was too worthless for anybody else to even bother with me, how could I cheat?

"Why are you working all the time? I'm gonna be leaving for boot camp in a few weeks and you're at work every day. Don't you wanna be with me? I mean, you're pretty lucky to be with me. I don't really even know why I'm worried about you cheating, nobody else would want you, since you're used goods."

I felt dirty. My breaths were shallow. I needed to get away from him. My heart was racing. "I have to get to work." Flat, emotionless.

I walked out of the bathroom, out of the house and drove to work. I got there early, and sat in the car, trying to focus on when I would be away from him, taking deep breaths to calm down. I escaped from Jay for the moment and kept myself from having a full-blown panic attack. I only had a few more weeks to go until he left for boot camp and I would be free. Maybe there was a glimmer of light in my dark life.

Chapter Twelve

I enjoyed my job. For the first time in my life, I felt useful and needed. I was just scooping ice cream, making sundaes and banana splits at first, but eventually they taught me how to frost and decorate ice cream cakes. I was valued and important. I wasn't constantly belittled there or told that I was doing everything wrong. I was often complimented on how well I accomplished my various tasks. It was addictive. I wanted to perform well, to keep my job, keep the compliments coming and save money. With money in the bank I would be able to escape my life.

Home, however, was just getting worse all the time. My mom was incredibly sick. The doctors still had absolutely no idea what was wrong with her. She was weak, tired and could barely eat. Stefyni and I took care of Keeth and each other. My grandma moved in to help with finances, but she ended up taking care of us because my mom wasn't able to. Grandma did our laundry and made us dinner. It was kind of nice to not have those responsibilities for once in my life. I had been making family meals since I was eight years old!

Unfortunately, my grandma didn't drive. That meant that when my mom was sick, which was a lot of the time, I had to drive Stefyni and Keeth around to school, friends' houses and appointments. I also had to do all the grocery shopping. The only time my mom went to the store was when she needed cigarettes because I was too young to buy them for her. It didn't matter that she was unable to eat, she could light up cigarette after cigarette like nothing. I hated it!

I hated that my clothes constantly smelled of smoke. I hated that my hair smelled like her cigarettes. I hated that the walls in our house were yellow with the chemicals in the smoke. I hated that she was too sick to take care of us. I hated that I had to go grocery shopping to make sure we ate, but she could pull herself together enough to go buy a carton or two of cigarettes. I hated that she couldn't afford to buy me clothes, but she could always afford more cigarettes. I hated that my bed was just a mattress on the floor because she couldn't afford a bed frame, but she always had enough for cigarettes.

I also hated that I had to use the money I was earning at work to pay for gas and lunch. Most of my driving was to go to school or drive my mom and siblings around to appointments and do errands, so I thought it was only right for my mom to pay for the gas. As for lunch, I firmly believe that parents should be sure that their child is eating. Having to pay for my own food and gas helped me get a taste of adulthood, that's for sure. I had to be careful with what I was earning and how spent it.

The first thing I saved money for was a bed of my own. At the time my bed was a mattress on the floor. Once I had some money saved I bought a white daybed with brass knobs. Jay helped me build it, then he expected that we'd "break it in." Lucky for me, my Grandma came to check on me and give me my clean uniform for work. Having grandma in the room killed his mood. I left him alone on my new bed, quickly changed for work in the bathroom, told him goodbye and left. I was extremely grateful for my ice cream scooping job.

I got my bed about a week before Jay left for boot camp. One day, when I returned home from school, he was sitting on my bed. "We need to talk."

"Okay. Let's talk." I sat down at the opposite end of the bed from him. I wanted to keep my distance.

"I'm leaving next week. I know you're still in high school and I'll be gone for three months." He began.

"Yeah." Could he possibly be breaking up with me? That would make everything so much better. "I know."

"I just want to tell you that I better not get a Dear John letter while I'm in basic."

"A what?" I had no idea what he was talking about.

"It's a letter a girl writes to break up with her boyfriend while he's off serving in the military."

He wasn't breaking up with me. He was instructing me not to break up with him. "Oh. I wasn't planning on writing you a Dear John letter." I'd start it with 'Dear Jay,' I told myself. I wasn't nearly brave enough to say it out loud to him.

"If I get a letter like that, I don't know what I'd do to you, but you better believe I'd go AWOL to come back here and find you."

"Okay, I get it." Why did he always have to threaten me?

"Besides, if you break up with me, nobody else would want you." While he spoke, he moved closer to me. "I mean look at you. You're such a tomboy." He waved his arm over my body. "You have no boobs." He flicked my breasts through my shirt. "You don't wear makeup." He touched my cheek. "You're lucky to have me." He leaned in and kissed me.

I hated him for treating me like crap. I hated myself for allowing it.

"I have to get ready for work. I get off at seven o'clock tonight."

"I'll pick you up at 7:15 for dinner. Did you get Sunday off so we can have a nice dinner before I leave on Monday morning?"

"Yes, I did." I replied without emotion.

"Good girl." As if I were a child following directions. "Have fun at work, but no flirting with any one."

"Thanks. See you later." I left. I couldn't wait for him to leave. I was too afraid to break up with him while he was here, but I hated how I felt when I was with him. He constantly put me down, called me 'Mitch,' which I hated, told me what to do, and did things to me I didn't want to do. He always seemed to be just on the verge of hitting me whenever I talked back or did something he didn't approve of.

I also didn't want to disappoint my mom by breaking up with him. As much as I felt like I had given up trying to earn her approval, I still wanted it. I still wanted her to love and support me and she supported me in my relationship with Jay. I liked her supporting me, I just wish it wasn't with Jay.

I wanted to be able to break up with him, but I was so worthless and weak, the battle it would take was overwhelming. Even another week seemed an eternity though. I was tired of being treated like a child. I was tired of having my body used for his pleasure. I just wanted to move on without him, but I knew that would be difficult too.

At work that day I was distracted by thoughts of a better future for myself. I calculated how much I would need to work in order to buy some of the items I thought I'd need to survive on my own. I had already purchased a bed, but I'd still need my own car to get around. Then I would need insurance. I also needed to pay for graduation stuff as a senior.

When my shift was over, I clocked out and headed home. Just as promised, Jay was there to take me to dinner. He had probably never left and just visited with my mom and Grandma. They both absolutely adored him. It made me want to vomit. He was so nice and charming around others, and then with me he was condescending and controlling. He seemed to have two sides to his personality, the one everyone else saw and the one I experienced.

I guess that was no different than me. When people were around I acted as though everything was fine and life was good, but on the inside I was falling apart and my life wasn't worth the effort it required. I would wear a smile for the world to see, when all I really I wanted to do was scream and cry and give up. I wouldn't give up though. I was not a quitter. I wanted to make something of myself in the future. I could make it happen if I could just get away from Jay.

We went to dinner and he brought me straight home afterwards because I had school the next day. When I came home, my mom was waiting for me in her usual spot on the living room couch. "How was dinner?"

"Alright." I was vague and uninterested in having a conversation with her.

"Do you still have homework?"

"No." I answered shortly.

"Good. Sit down and talk to me." She patted the couch cushion beside her.

I sat down on the couch opposite her.

"Jay is leaving on Monday for boot camp." She began the conversation.

"Yeah." I nodded.

"He's worried that he's going to get a Dear John letter from you."

"He already told me not to send him one." I couldn't believe he got her in on this. They were ganging up against me.

"I don't think you should break up with him. He's a good guy. You're not ever going to find someone as good as him. He's going in the military. He'll make a decent living. He'll be able to take care of you."

I was getting nauseous. I hated when she talked to me about what a great person Jay was. If she only knew what he was really like. I wanted to scream, "He makes me have sex with him every chance he gets," but all I said was "I know."

"He asked me to keep an eye on you. To make sure you don't send him a Dear John letter. And to make sure you write to him every day. He's really gonna miss you" She was laying it on thick.

All he'll miss is telling me what to do and using me to pleasure himself. "Whatever. I'm going to bed now. School in the morning. Good night." I walked quickly down the hallway to get away from her and the conversation. Jay was leaving, but he had already made sure I knew he had a spy.

"Good night." She said to my retreating back.

Why did life have to be so difficult? Why couldn't I have a normal family who just loved me all the time? A family where I didn't have to feel like I was always working to get my parents' acceptance. Was being loved, just for being me, so hard for people to do? I was tired of trying all the time. Being good all the time was exhausting.

I laid there and tried to sleep as these thoughts continued to race through my mind. It was hard to turn my mind off so I could sleep. Tears rolled down my cheeks to my pillow. I hugged my little green blanket as I tried to calm my mind. Sleep eventually came and I dreamed about having my own life away from Jay and my mom. It was a great dream, but it was only a dream.

Chapter Thirteen

It was a typical Sunday, except that Jay was leaving, without Dustin who decided not to join, the next morning for basic training for the Marines. People at school and church told me I should be so proud to be dating a Marine, and such a great guy too. My mind continued to replay the first time he forced me to have sex. The look in his eyes when he said he was done just messing around. The look that told me I had no choice, I was his to do whatever he wanted to. The look that made me feel completely and utterly worthless.

The more I thought about what kind of person Jay really was in comparison to who people thought he was, the more depressed I got. Tears filled my eyes, threatening to run down my face. People thought I was upset that he was leaving. They offered hugs of support. It was a sham. None of them cared about me. Not really.

I spent the afternoon at Jay's house. It was a typical day with Jay. We went to lunch after church, then went back to his house, where he led me to his bedroom. To his bed.

"God, I'm going to miss this!" as he kissed my neck and unbuttoned my pants. "I need a good one to remember you by."

I let him do what he wanted to do. I followed his directions to make sure he was happy.

"MMMM. That was amazing! I'm definitely going to think about that to get me through the next three months. I'll take you home now so you can clean up for our date."

"Can't wait." I said. I could wait for dinner; I couldn't wait for him to leave. I needed to start living my life, but I was scared. When he was around I was useless and worthless. I got dressed and we left for my house.

He walked me to the door. "I'll be back at five o'clock. I have reservations for five-thirty." He leaned in and kissed me on the forehead. "Make sure you look good."

"I'll do my best." I promised as I went in the front door.

"Welcome home, Mishell. What do you need to get ready for tonight?" My mom asked as soon as I walked in the door.

I didn't want to talk to her. I still felt dirty from having sex with him just a few minutes ago. "I have to shower, do my hair and makeup."

"What are you wearing?" She seemed very interested in this date.

"Jay bought a dress for me to wear. I have to wear that one." I answered.

"That was nice of him. He really takes good care of you, doesn't he?" She was trying to remind me about what a good guy he was.

"I guess." I thought it was his way of making sure I was presentable. That I was wearing what he knew he'd like. At least at dinner, I could relax and know that there'd be no sex afterwards. He'd already done that today.

"I don't know what's wrong with you lately, Mishell. You act like nothing matters. You better not screw things up with Jay. He's gonna be the one to take care of you."

"I know, I know. I gotta get in the shower." With that I stood and walked away from my mom. I was so irritated. She had no clue what she was talking about. I needed someone to help me escape from her and Jay. It's like they're a team against me. He manipulated her to control me.

I turned the water on as hot as I could handle it. I wanted to wash off every reminder of Jay. This was the last time that I would have to deal with him forcing me to have sex with him. Once he was gone, that part of my life would be so much easier. I scrubbed until my skin felt raw. When I got out of the shower, I slathered on lotion to comfort my skin. I put on pajamas to get ready. I'd wait to put the dress on until the last minute so that I didn't get make up or hair spray on it.

I attempted to curl my hair, but I wasn't very good at it, however, it was presentable. Then I put eye shadow and blush on. When I was done with all that, I had about thirty minutes before he would be there. When I put the dress on, I did feel pretty, but I didn't feel like me. It wasn't the kind of dress I would have picked at all. It had a purple paisley print, a very low neckline, and mid length sleeves. It was knee length and I wore it with white flats.

"Mishell, show me the dress." I heard from the living room.

I didn't want to show her because the cigarette smell would get into my dress. "I'll be right there." I ran my hands down the front of my dress to smooth out any wrinkles and walked to the living room.

"You look beautiful. Jay is really gonna like it."

I smiled in response. Of course he will, he bought it, I said to myself. It didn't matter to me if Jay liked it or not. I wouldn't have to see him after this.

"I really hope you know how much Jay needs you while he's in basic training. It's gonna be hard for him and he needs to know that you're here waiting for him." She never stopped being his cheerleader.

"I know. He already told me that."

"I just want to make sure you don't do something you'll regret later."

She had no idea that I did things with Jay that I already regretted. "I know, Ma! You're always looking out for our best interest. Right?"

"Glad you finally understand. Have a good time at dinner. Remember to be a lady."

"Always." Dripping with sarcasm.

Just then the door opened and in walked Jay. He looked good in his black slacks with a perfect crease, his button up shirt and tie. "Hey Mitch. Ready?"

"Yep. Let's go!" I exclaimed with faked enthusiasm.

"I'm really going to miss you while I'm gone. I love you so much, Mishell. I don't know what I'd ever do without you. You're lucky to have me too. I know it's gonna be hard for you while I'm gone."

I shrugged my shoulders. "I guess."

"I won't be here for your Junior Prom, that's why I wanted tonight's dinner to be fancy. I don't want you to feel like you're missing something since you can't go to the prom."

I hadn't even thought about the prom and whether I would go or not. "That's really sweet of you. Thanks!" I smiled. It was sweet. He was capable of being nice, just enough to string me along. I knew what he was really like by this time and he wasn't fooling me any longer.

"Jay, your table's ready. Please follow me." The hostess interrupted us.

We followed her through the restaurant to a semi-private booth with high seats that separated us from the diners at the next table. "Here you go." She waved towards the table. As I slid in on one side, she handed me a menu, "A menu for you. And one for you." Handing one to Jay. "Your server will be right with you."

We looked over the menu. The server brought us water, took our order and promised our dinner would be right out.

Jay reached for my hands across the table. "I want tonight to be special, Mishell. I feel bad that I'll miss your Junior Prom."

"Don't worry about it. I haven't even thought about it." It was truth.

"I want you to know that while I'm gone, I'll be thinking about you every day. It'll make all the torture I'm going to go through easier, knowing that you're here waiting for me."

I smiled nervously. He had no idea what I was planning. "What are you looking forward to learning in boot camp?"

"Learning to be a sniper. I want to get good at shooting targets. Then when I go to war, I can kill 'em all."

That was a little scary. He was looking forward to learning to kill people. "Really?"

"Yeah. Then if anybody tries to take you away from me while I'm gone, I can take care of him." He said matter-of-factly.

I was speechless. There was nothing I could say to that. He truly frightened me. He had raised his hand to hit me enough times, that I was surprised that he hadn't hit me yet. If he'd have hit me instead of having sex with me, it would be easier to break up with him. Being hit was not as humiliating as being forced to have sex.

Maybe I wouldn't be able to break up with him while he was gone. What if he came back and was mad at me? What would he do to me then? I began to rethink my strategy.

"What are you thinking about, Mishell? You're being quiet."

"I'm just thinking about what I'll do when you're gone. I'll have time to hang out with Shauna again. And I'll stay busy with work." I was looking forward to a life without him here.

"As long as you don't stay so busy you don't have time to write to me every day." He replied.

"Every day?" That seemed over the top to me.

"I'll need to know that you're home waiting for me. Knowing that you're waiting for me will make it so much easier for me to get through basic. When things are hard I'll think of you. Getting a letter from you every day will let me know you're waiting."

"I'll do my best." I lied.

Just then the server came with our dinner. We ate in relative silence. Jay didn't like to talk while he ate. He wanted to savor his food. Especially his last meal before military food. My mind was racing. I kept a calm façade, but inside I was falling apart. Breaking up with him when he left was looking more and more difficult. He was already setting me up to control me while he was gone. And he had threatened to come after me if I did break up with him. I was still trapped in this horrible, dangerous relationship.

Saying goodnight was bittersweet. I knew that he would miss me and in a way, I would miss him too. My mom allowed me so much freedom to go places with Jay and I enjoyed that freedom. I hoped it would continue after he left tomorrow. I did have my license now and she had me run all the errands, which gave me time away from home.

I would also miss the times that Jay made me feel good even though they were few and far between. I learned to put up with the bad stuff because every once in a while he could be exceptionally sweet and loving towards me. I learned a long time ago that when someone loves you, you deal with the bad treatment in between the good stuff. It was the way life worked, at least in my family.

He kissed me at the door. It was an early night, I had school in the morning and he had to catch a bus to San Diego. He hugged like he didn't want to let me go. I was conflicted. I liked when he treated me well, like now, but I hated when he treated me as his property, telling me what to do and who I could do it with.

We said good night, I walked in my house and leaned on the door to close it. It was the last time that I would have to see him for three months. A glimmer of hope.

"Are you okay, Mishell? Are you going to survive without him?" My mom asked as soon as I closed the door.

"I'll be fine." I answered, sharply. I actually believed I might just be okay; things might eventually be fine. I just had to keep working and saving to escape from my family. It might take a while, but I'd be fine, someday. Maybe when I escaped, my mom would finally be proud of me and my accomplishments and love me for me. I could hope, right?

I slept well that night. It was the first night in a very long time that I fell asleep easily, slept all night and woke up refreshed. It was the first day of a brand new Mishell.

Chapter Fourteen

I woke up feeling rested and ready to face the day at school. Jay was heading to San Diego for three months of basic training and I had school, a job and friendships to rekindle. I had allowed a lot to slip by the wayside while dating Jay. My grades slacked and my friendships suffered. Feeling used and worthless sapped my energy and left me too empty to do anything other than survive.

I thought I was ready to face the first day in my new life away from Jay, but as soon as I arrived at school I was immediately overwhelmed with feelings of worthlessness. I was helpless and incapable of doing anything. It took every ounce of my energy to make it through first period. By the time I got to my second period history class, I couldn't hold it together any longer. I collapsed into my chair, put my head on my folded arms on the desk and cried.

Shauna sat behind me and patted my back, trying to calm me down, to no avail. The teacher passed out the test we were taking that day. I took mine, but did nothing with it, I just continued crying. I was unable to focus on anything beyond my own hopelessness and worthlessness.

Eventually the teacher came to me, "Mishell, are you okay?"

I didn't raise my head, just moved it back and forth, hoping he'd realize I was saying no.

"Are you going to take this test?"

I gave him the same non-verbal response.

"Why don't you take your things and go to the office. Talk to your counselor. I'll get you a pass." He was trying to be helpful, but I didn't want to talk to anyone.

I didn't want to sit in class crying either though so I gathered my backpack and purse and walked out of the classroom, straight to the office. I ended up getting in to talk to my counselor. I couldn't grasp what she was trying to tell me. The voice in my head kept telling me what I was.

    Whore.
    Slut.
    Hopeless.
    Idiot.
    Freak.
    Failure.
    Useless.
    Unimportant.
    Weak.
    Worthless.
    Over and over.

    Those words defined who I was. I didn't want to be those things anymore, but I didn't know how to change. I had great plans, but I was too weak to follow through. I hadn't even made it half a day without Jay and I was a sobbing mess. Why did I think that I could be better than those defining words?

    I left the office and somehow survived the rest of the day without another meltdown. I arrived home and was greeted by my mom.

    "Did you write to Jay yet? You know he'll be expecting a letter. It'd be nice for him to get a letter in the next few days, you know right after he gets there, to let him know you're supporting him." She was Jay's biggest fan.

    "Not yet." I grumbled.

    "You should go start that. I have envelopes and stamps if you need them."

    "Um, I have to go to work." I didn't, but I needed to leave.

    I parked in the lot at my work, pulled out some paper and began a letter to Jay. I wrote lies that he expected to hear. That I already missed him, couldn't wait for him to come back. Told him half-truths about my day at school. That I had a history test and saw my counselor. And truths, like my mom missed him and wanted him to do well.

When I was done writing the letter, I sat alone in my car in a crowded parking lot and cried. Not because Jay was gone, but because I didn't know who I was. I had worked so hard for so long being who my parents, friends and Jay expected me to be, to earn their love and acceptance that I had lost myself. I believed their lies about me. I believed that's who I was. I didn't know how to be me anymore.

I knew my plan to graduate, save money, go to college and do something with my life was a good one, but I didn't know how I'd manage to do all of it. It seemed a daunting task looming in front of me. I wanted to be a nurse, like my mom, but I wasn't doing well in my math and science classes, but I knew I could survive on my own as a nurse, it was a good-paying profession. I'd just have to buckle down, do well and make my escape.

I had to leave the parking lot and face my mom eventually, so I started the car and drove home. As soon as I walked through the door, my mom started in at me from her permanent position on the living room couch. "How was work? Did you get a letter started? Do you have homework?"

"Oh my God! Ma! Please stop!" Frustrated. Irritated.

"What is wrong with you?" She snapped at me.

"I don't know. Just...ugh! I wrote Jay a letter. Happy now? Will you leave me alone about Jay now?" I wanted to go to my room, curl up in a ball and go to sleep for the next two years. "Do you have a stamp so I can mail it? I have to keep you and Jay happy."

"In my purse. Hold on" She dug through and handed one to me. "You better change your attitude really quick if you want to keep driving." She always threatened me with that. She'd never take the car away from me though. I was the only driver in the house.

"Thanks." I snatched the stamp out of her hand and affixed it to the envelope, walked across the street and dropped it in the outgoing mail slot. I returned to the house, walked past my mom, and down the hall to my room. Once I was in the safety of my bedroom, I stripped down to my t-shirt and underwear, crawled in bed, and curled into a ball under my covers where I stayed safe in my cocoon until my alarm went off for school the next morning.

I saw Shauna in history class. "Hey Mishell. Feeling better today?"

"I guess." I shrugged.

"Wanna stay the night this weekend? You haven't been able to stay over since you started dating Jay. We can go out cruising or to a movie or something. I have my mom's car."

"That'd be fun. I'll ask my mom and let you know." I said it with a little more enthusiasm than I felt. It sounded fun, I had never been cruising. Jay thought the idea of driving your car up and down the same street was idiotic, so we never went. It sounded a whole lot better than staying at home with my mom who would, no doubt, talk incessantly about Jay, on my night off.

The rest of school that day was a blur. It was difficult to focus on classes, but was looking forward to a night out with Shauna. I knew I wasn't her best friend anymore, but she was still the closest thing I had to a best friend. It was nice of her to try to cheer me up and make sure I was doing okay.

When I walked through the front door to my house that afternoon, my mom didn't bombard me with questions about Jay or how my day was. It was a relief, but I had to initiate a conversation. I sat down on the sofa across from where my mom sat in her permanent spot in the corner of the couch.

"Can I stay the night at Shauna's this Friday? I don't have to work."

"What are the plans?" She questioned, ever the dutiful mother, as if I'd tell her the truth.

"Just to hang out like we did before I started dating Jay. Remember when you used to let me stay the night there. We'll probably watch a movie or something like that." I didn't want to tell her we were going cruising, because she'd never allow it, she thought it was too dangerous.

"I suppose so, as long as you do all your chores and go grocery shopping first. You can drive yourself." I hadn't expected her to drive me, she hadn't driven in months.

"Thanks, Ma." I went to my room and started homework looking forward to the first weekend without Jay.

The rest of the week was successful in that I didn't have another meltdown and I was able to focus more in class, but I was still confused on who I really was and what I wanted to do. I didn't want to be Jay's girlfriend anymore, but I was worried about upsetting my mom and scared of what he'd do, so I kept writing to him. I wrote him a letter every day that week. Even though I knew I didn't want to be with him, I didn't know how to be without him, yet.

Friday came and I had finished all my chores so I went to Shauna's house. We spent the afternoon lounging around her house. It was like the comfortable, relaxed, old times, before Jay. I enjoyed myself. I laughed until I cried. I didn't think about Jay, or what he would say about how I was behaving or my laughter. I just had fun.

In the evening, we got ready to go out. It felt good to not worry about what Jay or my mom would say about my clothes or hair. I didn't do anything special, jeans and a t-shirt, hair half up in a barrette, but I felt good about myself. Nobody was telling me what to do or how to look that night.

About eight o'clock we did a final once over of our looks, decided we both looked good, and climbed in her white Ford Tempo to head to Pacific Avenue. It was about fifteen minutes before we arrived at the avenue to cruise.

Neither of us had gone cruising before, we were excited about the prospect of driving up and down the street, with our windows down and music blaring, checking out the hot cars and the good-looking guys driving them.

I had a weakness for a particular car. I absolutely loved 1960s Ford Mustangs. I loved their sleek body style, the chrome accents and the growl of the engine. They were classic muscle cars that reflected strength, power, and endurance. I wished I had those same traits. I wanted the strength to stand against my mom and Jay. I longed for the power to stand up and figure out who I was as an individual. I hoped for the endurance to last through tough times instead of just giving up and giving in.

There were so many cars out there that we never got the speedometer over twenty miles per hour. We managed to get stopped at every intersection by a red light. It was cold with the windows down, so we had the heater full blast and the music up loud. We flirted with guys in other cars. It was the most fun I'd had in months and best of all there was no pressure to behave a certain way. After a few hours, we decided to head back to Shauna's house for the night.

I slept well that night. I fell asleep with hope that my life could be better; I just had to have the strength, power and endurance to make it happen. I had spent so many nights, crying, asking God to make my life better, but I was beginning to realize that God wasn't going to do it. It was up to me to make my life better. I didn't know exactly how I would do it. I knew I felt good about myself at work and that I had fun with Shauna. Those were good baby steps for me.

Chapter Fifteen

Over the next few weeks, I continued to write to Jay almost every day. If I didn't my mom hassled me, until one day she didn't. I didn't write to him that day, or the next. Next thing I knew a week had gone by without me writing to him. Shauna and I were hanging out more when I wasn't at work and I was making more friends in school. My mom still made me go to church, but I didn't feel like I needed to go to make God love me. I figured that He either loved me or He didn't. What we did or didn't do had no bearing on whether or not God loved us. My mom was just a religious freak in my eyes.

I had believed that dating a Christian was God's plan for my life, and look how that had turned out for me. I started dating Jay because he was a Christian and went to my church and in the beginning, had made me feel special and cared for. Once I did start dating him, for whatever reason, my mom acted like I was somebody too. She allowed me more freedom when I was dating Jay, but it didn't matter that they accepted me because I ended up feeling worse about myself.

Jay talked down to me and treated me as though I was his property, telling me who I could and couldn't talk to. He even checked on my grades at school to make sure I was doing well. That was a joke since he had dropped out of traditional high school and graduated from a continuation school, yet he thought my grades were important. He forced me to do things with him and to him sexually that I didn't want to do. I dated him to feel better about myself. That whole plan backfired on me.

I continued to work a lot. At work, I was learning to make and decorate ice cream cakes, which was a big responsibility. For them to teach me that meant that I was valuable to the employer. They wanted me to be there for the long term. The owner had even told me when he hired me that he didn't usually hire high school students because they tend to be flaky and immature, but I seemed mature to him so he took the chance. It was a boost to my self-image. I knew I wasn't where I wanted to be yet, but I was moving in the right direction.

I wrote to Jay less and less and Shauna and I went cruising more and more. One night while we were out I saw a 1965 Ford Mustang. It looked like it had been red at one point in the past, but had faded to orange paint with many spots covered in gray primer. We were on the right side of them so Shauna was close to the passenger side of the Mustang with her window rolled down.

She looked over at them and at the next stop light the passenger in the Mustang started talking to her. We decided to pull over in a parking lot to talk to them. She thought the passenger was especially cute. I hadn't paid too much attention to either of the guys in the car, I was looking at the car. It needed a lot of work on the outside, but the engine sounded good. I was impressed.

When we parked, they were still on the driver's side of Shauna's car. We got out of our respective cars. I walked around to the driver's side of our car, while their driver walked around to the passenger's side of his car. We introduced ourselves and found out that Paul was the driver and Tom was the passenger.

During our conversation, we discovered that they had graduated from our rival high school the spring before and they knew a few of our classmates. Even though I was enjoying myself, I couldn't stop thinking about what Jay or my mom would say if they knew that we had pulled over to talk to complete strangers. Jay would flip out and would probably threaten to hit me for it. My mom would call me a cheater because I was still dating Jay. I hadn't broken up with him yet, even though I was writing to him less. I was too scared to put the words into writing.

What if I broke up with him and he was right about the fact that no other guy would ever want to date me because I had sex with him? What if other guys thought that made me easy or a slut? I would rather stay with Jay and hope he changes than to be alone for the rest of my life. Besides, what if my mom was right and all teen-aged boys wanted was sex? If that were the case, what would be the point of leaving Jay for another guy who did the same exact thing to me?

I was continuously checking out the car while these thoughts raced through my mind and trying to be a part of the conversation. Eventually, Paul started talking about his car and all the work he had done and still had to do. I think it bored either Shauna or Tom because they changed the subject to possibly going on a date the next weekend. Shauna agreed as long as it was a double date with Paul and me tagging along. We hashed out the details and decided that Paul and Tom would pick up Shauna and me the next Saturday night at her house. I had the night off, so it would work and I had plenty of time to get permission.

The guys decided it was time to get back to cruising so we got back into our respective cars and drove away.

"I can't believe we not only pulled over with those guys, but we're going out with them next weekend." Shauna said as we pulled onto the street.

"Yeah, but I'm still dating Jay and you set me up for a double date with you."

"Oh yeah. You haven't been talking about him much." It seemed like she forgot I was still dating him.

"I think it'll be okay because I'm just going with you. It's not like I'm going on a real date with him. I just won't tell my mom or Jay." I reasoned.

"It'll only be this one date. If I go on a second date with Tom, it'll be by myself." She promised.

"Sounds good." I was nervous about our double date. It was a week away, but I was already wondering about whether Paul would like me or not. This could be my opportunity to see if another guy could like me. Then I could break up with Jay because I wouldn't be alone.

I worked hard all week justifying going on a date while my boyfriend was off in basic training. I was planning on breaking up with him after all, so it wasn't like I was cheating on him. Besides, I was only going on the date so that Shauna could get to know Tom better without having to be alone with him on the first, awkward date. By the time Saturday night rolled around, I was comfortable with going on a date without breaking up with Jay first and without telling him or my mom about the date.

Date night arrived, Shauna and I were ready and waiting for the boys to pick us up. They pulled into the driveway and walked to the door to get us. I thought Paul looked good. He was tall and thin with medium brown hair and amazing blue eyes. Tom and Shauna climbed into the back seat, Paul slid in behind the steering wheel and I sat shotgun. I had never been inside a Mustang before and I was busy checking everything out.

We went to dinner for the first part of the date. When we parked at the restaurant, I tried to open the door, but I couldn't figure out which handle to pull. "How do I get out of here?" I asked, laughing.

"Pull up on the handle." Paul answered.

Shauna was laughing in the backseat.

"Which one? There's two here."

"The one that's not for the window." Shauna answered, still laughing.

"Sorry, I've never been in a car like this before."

"You've never been in a Mustang?" Paul asked. "I thought you knew all about them."

"No, I just love them." I smiled at him.

During dinner, the conversation was typical, getting to know each other stuff. It was relaxed and comfortable. There were even a few jokes thrown in every now and then.

Once in the car after dinner, Tom asked, "do you guys mind if I have a cigarette before the movie?"

"Go ahead. Before we go in, but not in the car." Paul answered.

At the theater, Shauna and I went to the restroom. "So, what do you think, Shauna? Will there be a second date?"

"No. He smokes. I could never kiss a guy who smokes! It's disgusting!"

I just laughed, "I agree. It's so gross. I'm glad Jay doesn't smoke."

"Paul seems interested in you. Are you going to tell him about Jay?"

"You think he's interested in me? I don't know. He seems like a nice guy." I tried to sound like it didn't matter, but I was excited to think he was interested in me. It showed me that somebody besides Jay could like me, that I wasn't completely worthless.

We met the guys in the lobby and went in to the theater. The movie was about a woman whose husband was controlling and abusive. Not a great movie for a first date, but we didn't know that beforehand. There was a scene where the husband accuses his wife of allowing a man into their home while he's away. He proceeds to hit her, then tell her how sorry he is and how much he loves her before he leaves to go into town. He comes back with roses and a red negligee for her. He takes her by the hand and begins to kiss her, while taking off the dress she is wearing and putting the negligee on her. He leads her to the room, where they make love. He is facing away from the camera, but she is facing the camera.

Her eyes and facial expression show that she would like to be anywhere, but there in that moment. When he looks at her, the expression is quickly replaced by a smile.

A tear escaped my eye. I knew exactly how she felt. I knew what it was like to have sex with someone, just to keep from being hit by them. I knew what she felt when he accused her of having a man in the house while he was gone. I knew the anxiety she felt, not knowing if the interaction with him was going to be physically painful, emotionally painful or both.

I tried to stop the tears before anyone saw them, but Paul saw. I caught his eye as I was peeking to see if he saw me. He smiled reassuringly at me. No judgment, no condemnation, just a friendly, helpful smile.

The movie goes on to show the wife running away and starting a new life. Unfortunately for her, the husband tracks her down. At the end of the movie, he comes into her new home and she ends up shooting him. I wished that could be the ending with Jay. I was scared though, that he would come after me like the husband came after the wife. He truly frightened me. I was very quiet and solemn throughout the rest of the movie.

Somehow, after the movie, Paul and I ended up alone together. "Hey, are you okay?"

"I have a boyfriend. He's in the Marines." I blurted.

"Okay. So, I guess there's no second date." He tried to joke.

"He does that to me." I don't know why I was telling this person who was essentially a stranger to me, something that I hadn't told anybody. I was confiding in him my most shameful secret. I guess I needed to tell someone and he was in the right place at the right time. The way he looked at me when he had seen me cry during that scene showed that he genuinely cared and was worried about me.

"What does he do?" A quizzical expression shadowed his features.

"He doesn't hit me, but he's controlling, like that husband with the towels and he forces me to have sex with him." I was unable to stop it from escaping my lips, even as my mind was screaming, "no, don't say it!"

"You mean he rapes you?" Shocked.

"He's my boyfriend." I reply without answering his question.

"If he forces you to have sex with him, its rape. It doesn't matter if he's your boyfriend."

Shauna and Tom walked up then and my conversation with Paul ended there.

Rape. That's the word for it. The word I had been afraid to call it. The word I didn't want to say. Other people got raped, not good, Christian, girls. Boyfriends didn't rape their girlfriends. Christian guys didn't rape their girlfriends. Rape is when you force someone to have sex against their will. That is exactly what Jay had done to me, too many times to count.

I didn't like the word. I hadn't wanted to admit that's what he did to me. It was bad enough that he forced me to have sex with him, but to say the word, rape, made it all too real.

I was quiet on the drive home. I had too much on my mind to focus on conversation. I decided to stop writing to Jay. He wouldn't get a "Dear John" letter from me; he wouldn't get any letters from me.

My expression must have given my emotions away. Paul reached for my hand and held it reassuringly. He gave it a gentle squeeze as if to convey to me that I would be okay. I needed that support right then. My best friend Shauna, sitting in the back seat, whom I had known for five years, had no idea what I was dealing with at that moment. Then, here was Paul, a guy I only met the week before, didn't know hardly at all, who I had just told my darkest secret to. I must be at the end of my rope, ready to burst. I needed to talk to somebody and Paul was there when the dam opened.

When Paul dropped us off, he and I exchanged phone numbers. Shauna didn't give her number to Tom, I guess there'd be no second date there.

When we got into her house she began the third degree. "What are you doing? You gave him your number! What about Jay? You've been with him for like a year and half! That means nothing? And I saw you holding his hand! What was that about? You plan on cheating on Jay?"

She wasn't this loyal to Jay a week ago when she set me up on this double date with her. "No, I'm not going to cheat on Jay. I plan on breaking up with him, but I can't do it while he's at basic training. Besides, Paul was just being a friend. He was being supportive."

I couldn't tell her why I needed support. I didn't want anybody else to know what Jay did to me. I didn't even mean to tell Paul, after seeing that movie though, I was going to explode. I had to tell somebody, but nobody else would know.

I was ashamed and embarrassed that I had allowed him to do those things to me. I didn't break up with him when it all started, so I must have somehow been okay with all of it. I wasn't though. I just wanted someone to like me and make me feel special. My mom said that all guys were like that; they only wanted one thing and they would do whatever it took to get it.

There was also the fact that I had sex with Jay. Because of that nobody else would want to be with me. I wasn't a virgin and everything I learned from church and my mom was that guys only wanted to date girls that were virgins and saved themselves for marriage. I hadn't done that. I had allowed Jay to continue to violate me, just so I could feel loved and accepted.

How could God even still love me? I had allowed Jay to use my body for months. I bought into his justification that he wanted to marry me so having sex was okay, that God wouldn't mind. But deep down, I knew better. I knew that God wanted me to save myself for marriage and I hadn't done that.

I couldn't tell Shauna any of that. I couldn't tell my mom, or my sisters, or my pastor. I was too ashamed. Somehow though I had told Paul. In telling Paul, I felt relief for the first time in a long time. There might be hope for me after all. Maybe I could stand up to my mom and Jay and break up with him. I was still scared about what Jay would do when I finally did tell him that I didn't want to see him anymore, but I had a glimmer of hope.

It was satisfying to finally put a word to what Jay did to me. Rape. It made it seem more like it was his fault than mine. It was still hard to say though; I had been ingrained from a young age that "boys will be boys" and that it's up to the girls to make sure boys behave themselves. We need to make sure that we don't antagonize them by what we wear, the way we talk or anything. It would take time for me to wrap my head around the fact that what Jay did was his fault, not mine. I did let his behavior towards me continue for nine months. Really, he had been touching me in ways that made me uncomfortable from the very beginning of our relationship, but I tolerated it because I was so excited to have a boyfriend and have somebody like me. Now, I just felt terrible. I didn't take good enough care of myself; Jay raped me and it was my fault.

Chapter Sixteen

After that double date, I stopped writing to Jay, but I also didn't talk to Paul. I wasn't ready to talk to him again. I was afraid of what I would say to him. I didn't want him to know any more about Jay and how I felt about him and what he did to me.

One afternoon, when I came home from school, my mom was in her usual place at the end of the couch. Her pillows and blankets were stacked on the opposite end so she could easily make the couch into her bed. She had a bed in a room she shared with my Grandma, but didn't like to sleep there. As soon as I closed the door behind me she asked me to sit down.

Grudgingly, I did as she asked. "What's going on?"

"I know you haven't been writing to Jay. He told me in a letter. He really wants you to come to his graduation from basic training. I bought us tickets for the flight and got a hotel. You and I are going to his graduation. I'll let him know that we'll be there and that you've been very busy with work and school so he doesn't feel bad for you not writing to him."

"I don't have a say in this?" I argued.

"I figured you were just busy and couldn't write to him. And I've already paid for everything so we're going. He's a great guy. What's going on with you?"

"Nothing. It's fine. I'll go. Whatever." They were teaming up against me and I lost the battle.

"You need to change your attitude. He's been nothing but nice to you. He's had patience with you while he's been gone and you haven't been writing him much. You need to be happy to see him when we get there." She demanded.

"I'll be so happy you won't even recognize me." I said sarcastically. "When are we going so I can ask for the days off work?"

She told me the dates. I went to change for work and left. When I got to work I requested the days off so I wouldn't get into trouble for not showing up. The boss allowed me three days off. One day to travel to San Diego, one day for the ceremony and one day to travel home. I was not looking forward to the trip. I had never flown before and I was anxious about that. I definitely did not want to see Jay. I didn't know what he'd do to me. At least my mom was going, he'd behave better with her there. He had to keep up the false identity that she knew.

A few days later, after school, I got in my car to go home. When I tried to start my car, the battery was dead. I didn't want to call my dad for help. I knew he'd be angry and he'd call me his favorite names; good-for-nothing-shit-for-brains, idiot, whore, etc. I wasn't in the mood to deal with that.

I still had Paul's phone number in my purse. I decided that it was worth a try. I went to the pay phone near the school office and dialed. God must have found a moment to smile on me because he answered the phone.

"Hello" He answered the phone.

"Hello. Is Paul there?" My voice shook, matching my trembling hands.

"It's me."

"This is Mishell."

"I know; I recognize your voice."

I smiled. My heart took flight. He recognized my voice "I don't know if you can help me, but my car battery died and I was wondering if you would… if you had jumper cables?" I nervously asked him.

"I can. I'll be right there. Are you in the high school parking lot?"

"Yep, with my sister. We'll wait for you. Thank you!" Relief washed over me, I wouldn't have to call my dad.

"See you soon. Good-bye." He said.

"Good-bye." My hands quit trembling when I hung up the phone.

Within ten minutes he showed up in his Mustang and took care of my car. While he was hooking the jumper cables up I talked to him. "Thank you for coming to do this. I could've called my dad, but he would yell at me and I don't want to deal with that. I really appreciate you doing this. I mean we haven't even talked since the other night. You didn't have to come do this, but thank you. I have to go to work soon so this is perfect." It all came rushing out, I paused to take a breath.

"Where do you work again?" He questioned, keeping up the small talk.

"The ice cream place on Hammer and West Lane." I informed him.

"Oh. I work at the grocery store around the corner from here." He paused for a minute while he turned the key in the ignition. "I got it started. The battery should charge while you drive it home and then it'll be fine."

"Thank you! You have no idea how much I appreciate you rescuing me." I gushed.

"You're welcome." He smiled at me as he got into his car.

My sister and I got in my car. She had been quietly watching the whole exchange.

"Who was that?" She demanded to know.

"That's Paul." I answered.

"No. Who is he?" She pressed.

"Someone that Shauna and I met cruising a few weeks ago. He knows about cars, so I decided to call him instead of your dad because I didn't want to get yelled at." I didn't want to explain any more to her.

"You know you're still dating Jay, right?" She seemed incredulous.

"Yes I know. And I'm going to see Jay graduate from boot camp next week." I was irritated by her accusatory tone. "Paul is just a friend."

"Good. It wouldn't be right if you cheated on Jay." She preached.

I remained silent for the drive home. I dropped her off and went to work.

A couple of days later, before I had to go to San Diego for Jay's graduation, Paul walked into the ice cream place where I worked. I was surprised to see him there. We talked while I waited on him and I learned that he liked vanilla ice cream with peanut butter on top, covered in chocolate syrup. I couldn't make him an ice cream like that at work, but I was getting to know more about him.

I took my break and sat with him while he ate his ice cream. I let him know that my mom was making me go to Jay's graduation and that I hadn't told her, or anybody but him, about how Jay treated me and what he'd done to me. I still couldn't understand why it was so easy to talk to him. This was my deepest held secret, what I didn't want anybody to know, yet here I was, pouring my heart out to this person that I barely knew. He reassured me that it'd be alright and that I was strong enough to stand up to both of them.

I wasn't too worried about how Jay would treat me while I was in San Diego with him and my mom. He'd be on his best behavior while my mom was chaperoning us. He had an image to maintain with her and I was betting on that to be safe while I was there with him.

A couple of days before I was to leave for San Diego I went to see Paul at work. I wanted to say good bye to him before I left. I told him I was scared to fly and he explained the science behind flying, explaining to me how the plane stays in the air. It comforted me.

Even though I was nervous about flying and scared of Jay, I was excited to go to San Diego. I wanted to go to the beach and the zoo; two things I knew San Diego was famous for. When my mom and I got settled in our hotel I asked, "Can we go to the beach?"

"No, Mishell. I don't really feel very good. I just want to rest so I can feel better for the ceremony tomorrow." She explained.

"Then can I go walk around a little bit?" I was hopeful. I had always wanted to go to San Diego.

"No. It's not safe for a young girl to be walking around by herself. You'd just be asking to be raped or attacked if I let you go out by yourself." Over protective mom was showing in her words.

"Ma! Come on, please! I don't want to be stuck in this room for the whole weekend! I didn't come all the way to San Diego to see the inside of a hotel room!" I argued.

"No, you came to see your boyfriend graduate from boot camp. We're not going anywhere tonight." She came back at me.

Not wanting to make her too angry I conceded. "Fine. I'll stay in, but I want to do something tomorrow, please."

"We'll see."

"Where is Jay going to sleep?" I didn't want to share a bed with either of them.

"He can sleep on the floor, or you can sleep with me and he can have that bed. I guess that's up to you and him. You and Jay can't share a bed though." She was always looking out for me, or so she thought.

"I'll decide tomorrow." I clicked on the television and stopped talking. She eventually fell asleep. I watched television for a long time before I set my alarm for the morning and fell asleep too.

In the morning, after we got ready for the day, a cab picked us up to drive us to the military base for the graduation ceremony. When we arrived at the base, I was impressed with all the young men in uniform. The part of the base that we could see was decorated with American and Marine flags. There were units of well-trained young men marching in unison on the parade area. It was extremely impressive. For a moment I was proud to be dating a Marine. Then I remembered what he did to me and I went back to just being impressed by the order and cleanliness of the base and the Marines I saw.

My mom and I watched the ceremony from the grandstands. It was awe-inspiring and magnificent. I adored the meticulous marching and the grandeur of all of it. The ceremony was incredible. Hundreds of Marines, marching in unison. It was a sight I will never forget. I couldn't pick Jay out from the crowd, they all looked the same with their closely cut hair, dress blue uniforms and white hats. I didn't mind not knowing which one he was because it allowed me to enjoy the ceremony without distraction.

When the ceremony concluded, Jay found my mom and me in the grandstand. He walked right up to us and enveloped my mom in a big hug and thanked her for coming to his graduation. Then he turned to me, gave me a kiss and hug. I wanted to vomit. I didn't want him touching me, but I also didn't want to ruin his special day. I always found a reason not to stand up to him. At least my mom was there so I thought he'd treat me well.

Jay treated us to lunch on base before we went back to the hotel. My mom allowed him and me to walk around near the hotel and to go to dinner. The hotel was located in the Gas Lamp area of San Diego and was interesting to see. The streets were lined with historic buildings; I wish I knew all the stories to go along with them. I enjoyed the walk.

He chose a Mexican restaurant for dinner, his favorite, but I didn't mind, it was good food. I wasn't completely hating the afternoon with him. He was treating me nicely and, I thought, appropriately. We took some food back for my mom, she was sleeping when we got to the room.

We put her food in the mini refrigerator in the corner of the room. Jay went to take a shower and I watched television. While Jay was still in the shower, my mom woke up. "How was the afternoon? Did you get to do all you wanted?"

"It was nice. These old buildings are really cool. We brought you come dinner. Rice and beans." I was trying to be pleasant.

"Thank you. Where is Jay going to sleep?"

"I haven't talked to him about it yet. I will when he gets out of the shower." Just then he emerged from the bathroom. "Jay, do you want to sleep on the floor and I get the bed, or you get this bed and I sleep with my mom?"

"I'll sleep on the floor. Don't want to make your mom share her bed with you."

"What a gentleman!" My mom exclaimed.

I knew it was just a show for her so I remained silent on the matter. "I'm going to put jammies on now." I grabbed my stuff off the chair next to the window and walked into the bathroom to change.

Even though the walk and dinner with Jay had been pleasant, he didn't touch me or in any way make me feel uncomfortable, I was having a difficult time being with him in the room. When we were out I could be distracted by the architecture of the buildings in the area. The Gaslamp District is the historic area of San Diego. The buildings are old, brick structures; some with Spanish flair. It was all so beautiful! Now, in the room, all there was to distract me was the television and my mom and she had no idea that she needed to be distracting me, in fact she kept trying to get me to talk to Jay instead of watch television. I was miserable.

At one point, my mom went into the bathroom and Jay whispered, "When she falls asleep, I'm climbing in bed with you. I haven't been with you in months and I can hardly stand it."

I didn't know how to respond. I thought that I would be safe with my mom in the room with me. I didn't think that I would have to fight him off while we were in San Diego. "Not going to happen." I laughed nervously.

He ran his fingers from my forehead, down my cheek to my neck and across my chest, pausing over each breast as he moved. "All I have been thinking about for the past three months is being with you again. I can't wait much longer." He took his hands off me, just as my mom emerged from the bathroom.

"I think I'm going to sleep now." I announced to the two of them. If I was sleeping, he wouldn't be able to do anything to me.

"Why so early, Mishell?" My mom asked.

"I didn't sleep well last night," I lied. "I'm really tired from that and walking around all afternoon. Good night, Ma. Good night, Jay" I slipped under the covers, turned away from Jay and snuggled the blanket under my chin.

"Good night." They responded in unison.

As I lay there with my eyes closed, slowing my breaths to sound asleep, all I could think was that I was just avoiding confrontation. I hated thinking that anybody was mad at me. I would allow myself to be mistreated just to keep people liking me. It had brought me to this point. Faking sleep, just to avoid my boyfriend, who I didn't want to be with anymore. I hated myself and wanted to change. I wanted to feel valued and loved by somebody and no matter how many sacrifices I made in this relationship, I still didn't feel valued or loved.

Apparently, I fell asleep because I woke up to my mom's alarm. She reached for it and turned it off, but not before Jay and me both woke up. He was lying on the floor. I was relieved. He had been sitting next to me when I faked sleep last night. She rolled off the bed and stumbled around the room, digging her clothes out of her luggage. When she accomplished the task, she disappeared into the bathroom. I heard the toilet flush and the shower turn on.

As soon as the shower was on, Jay was in bed with me. He was naked. No wondering what his plan was. "No Jay. My mom is here."

"So. She's in the shower. She'll never hear us." He tried removing my shirt.

I swatted at his hand, "I don't want to with my mom here. I don't want her to catch us."

He left my shirt alone and went for my shorts. "It's been so long. I need you. If I don't have sex with you right now, I might just explode."

"What about protection?" I tried stalling the inevitable.

"What, you don't want to have my baby?" He asked acting hurt.

"No. Please, Jay!" I pleaded. It was pointless. He pinned me down, took my shorts off, moved my panties to the side and did what he wanted with me.

I felt just like the character in the movie I had seen with Paul, when her husband leads her to their bed and had sex with her. You could see she wasn't enjoying it and neither was I. A single tear escaped my eyes and forged a trail down my cheek into my hair. He finished and looked expectantly at me. I smiled at him, avoiding confrontation. Inside I wanted to scream and cry and tell him what I thought of him, but I was weak. Scared. Silent.

Jay rolled off me as my mom turned off the shower in the bathroom. He pulled his shorts back on and moved back to his spot on the floor. I stayed in bed, fixed my panties, pulled my shorts back on and turned away from Jay. I pulled the blankets up to my chin, trying to hide in a cocoon of blankets and started to silently cry. I had let him do it again. The words flooded my mind.

Slut.
Whore.
Good-for-nothing.
Weak.
Useless.
No good.
Idiot.
Tramp.
Worthless.

As the words continued to race through my mind, I succeeded in stopping the tears. By the time my mom emerged from the bathroom, I was faking sleep again. I couldn't face her. I couldn't face him. I was a horrible human being.

I had to eventually face both of them. I talked myself into getting up and ready. I showered quickly because we had to catch a cab to the airport. Even though it was a quick shower, it was as hot as I could stand to try to sanitize myself. I hated that he had been in me and left a part of himself in me. I tried my best to clean every lingering trace of him away.

I still felt dirty when I stepped out of the shower. I attempted to cover up the invisible filth with my clothes and exited the bathroom. Jay went in to shower when I came out. My mom called the cab. When Jay was showered, we grabbed our luggage, checked out in the lobby and waited for the cab to arrive. I was quiet and withdrawn. Neither of them seemed to notice as they carried on their own conversation without me.

Chapter Seventeen

I made a plan for breaking up with Jay on the flight home. He would be home for a week before leaving again for his next training school. I would bide my time and attempt to stay away from him. With school and work, it'd be pretty easy, especially since I had to miss a few days of school for his graduation so I would have a lot of work to make up. Besides, he would want to hang out with some of his other friends too, that would give me a reprieve from him as well.

When Dustin and I took him to catch his flight back to San Diego, I would give him the letter that I had avoided writing while he was in basic training. The letter I was scared to give him because I didn't know how he'd react; if he'd just yell or if he'd finally hit me. He had threatened to do just that plenty of times before and it frightened me to think that someday he'd follow through with his threats.

It wouldn't be that difficult to pretend for one more week. I tried to convince myself, but I knew it would be hard. He'd want to have sex whenever we were alone together, so I had to make sure that didn't happen. I could try to keep Dustin with the two of us whenever we were together.

I was confident that I would be able to carry out my plan. I just had to keep the negative thoughts away. I had to keep the words out of my mind that threatened every second of everyday to hold me down in the depths of despair. It was going to be easier said than done, but if I was going to survive this life, I needed to make some changes and getting Jay out of my life was the first one.

Throughout the week I managed to not be alone with Jay. I was successful in keeping him from using me again. The night before Jay had to leave, Dustin went to dinner with Jay and me. It was nothing fancy or special, just a last chance to see each other before he shipped out again in the morning. Jay had no idea, what I was planning to give him in the morning; I just hoped I would have the courage to carry it out.

After dinner, we went back to Jay's house and watched a movie. When the movie was over, Jay announced, "Time for you to go home, Mishell."

I knew, because Dustin told me, that often before Jay went to basic training, he and Dustin would go do things after he dropped me off at home. Sometimes they drank, smoked, went and threw pennies at hookers, nothing good. I didn't want him to go do something stupid with Dustin and get a ticket or citation because then he wouldn't be allowed to go back to the Marines.

I don't know where the courage or strength came from. "I'll only leave if Dustin leaves too." I stated.

As soon as the words were out of my mouth, Jay pulled his arm back and landed his open palm on my cheek. It stung. "You hit me!" I shrieked.

"You made me do it! Who the hell do you think you are to tell me what to do? I tell you what to do." He spat at me.

Without another word, I walked to my car and drove home. That was it. Being slapped was what needed to happen so I could tell my mom that I was breaking up with Jay. Not that I was happy about it. When I looked in the rear-view mirror as I drove, even in the dim light of the street lamps, I could make out his palm print on my right cheek. It was tender to my touch.

Luckily, my mom was asleep when I got home so I didn't have to tell her anything that night and have her try to talk me out of it. I could have that conversation with her after I had given Jay the letter in the morning. I went straight to my room and started the writing.

Dear Jay,

I promised you I wouldn't write you a "Dear John" letter, so I'm not. This is a "Dear Jay" letter, but you're still not going to like it.

I'm breaking up with you. I was already planning on it, but you hitting me was the icing on the cake.

You raped me. I can't forgive you for that. You forced me to have sex with you against my wishes. I'm done.

Mishell

That was it, short and to the point. I went to bed and slept fitfully, scared of how he would react.

Early the next morning, Dustin picked me up and together we went to get Jay.

"Dustin, I have a letter I want to give Jay, but I don't want him to read it while I'm still there. Can we leave as soon as I give it to him please? I also would appreciate it if you would drive me to school this morning." My hands fidgeted with the letter in the pocket of my hooded sweatshirt.

"Whatever you need. What's in the letter?" He asked.

"I'd rather not say yet, but I can tell you later. After I give it to him" I promised.

"Okay." He didn't press it any further.

We drove the rest of the way in silence. I'm sure that Dustin was dying to know what the letter said. I was dreading Jay's reaction when he read it, but I was relieved that this nightmare relationship would be over. If my plan worked, I'd be in the parking lot before he read it.

Jay was waiting outside when we pulled into his driveway. I got out and moved to the backseat and Jay took the front. "Good morning, Mitch."

I cringed. I still hated that name from him. "Morning."

"What's wrong with you?" He asked me.

"Nothing. Just tired." I lied. I didn't want to upset him again, giving him another opportunity to hit me.

"When you left last night, you were mad. Are you all better now?" His voice dripped with condescension.

I rolled my eyes, in the dark he couldn't see, "I'm fine." I said through clenched teeth.

He didn't respond to me, but started a conversation with Dustin.

He dismissed me again. It was the last time he would do that. I reached into my pocket and felt the letter there, folded into a neat rectangle. I couldn't wait to give it to him, but I would run away as soon as I did.

When we arrived at the small local airport it was still dark outside. The lights inside momentarily blinded me. I squinted as my eyes transitioned to the brightness.

"What's wrong? Lights to bright for you? So weak." Jay teased. "I learned how to handle all kinds of situations like this. I'm a Marine!" He was so proud of himself.

I waited a few minutes before announcing, "I need to go so I can get to school on time. Dustin, are you ready?"

"Yep."

Jay came over to me and wrapped his muscular arms around me. I remembered when he first did that in my driveway a year and a half before and I felt lucky, loved and safe. Now I felt trapped. He leaned down and kissed me, for the last time. "Bye, Mitch. Hope you do a better job of writing me this time."

"I already started. Just, please, don't read it until I leave." I handed him the letter.

"I'll try to wait." He replied.

He leaned in to kiss me, I turned so his lips landed on my cheek. "Gotta go!"

I walked towards the parking lot as fast as my little legs could carry me; Dustin had a hard time keeping up. His car would take me away from there and to safety.

We got to his car and Dustin started the ignition. "What's the hurry?" he asked me.

"Please, Dustin. Just go. I don't want him to find me after he reads the letter." My voice cracked as I spoke.

He backed out of the parking spot and drove away. "Why? What did the letter say?"

"I broke up with him." My voice was just above a whisper.

"You did what? Why?" He turned to look at me.

"Keep your eyes on the road please!" Becoming more confident I answered him, "Because he hit me and it's not okay for him to hit me."

"I guess that's fair. But you're going to throw away the past year and a half because he hit you last night?" He was asking the same questions I thought my mom would ask.

"Absolutely. He shouldn't have done that to me. I did nothing to deserve it." Staring straight ahead.

"You did challenge his authority." Dustin countered.

"By not wanting him to go out and do something stupid with you. Besides, why does he get to tell me what to do, but I don't get to tell him? I'm a person, not his property." I glared at him.

"You are his girlfriend." He stressed the word 'are.'

"Not anymore, I'm not. Besides, being his girlfriend doesn't mean that he's the boss of me." My voice was growing stronger. "Please, take me to school now. I'm done talking about this."

School was a blur that day. I went from class to class, did what I was supposed to do, but my heart wasn't in it. I couldn't focus on anything except that I was free from my abuser. Well, as long as he went to his training, as long as he didn't come back and come after me, as long as he accepted that I broke up with him. It was hard to believe that I was truly free from him, but I was going in the right direction.

On my way home from school that afternoon, I stopped at the grocery store where Paul worked. He was bagging groceries so I made sure he saw me then went outside to wait by his Mustang for him. A few minutes passed before he came out to gather shopping carts and to find out why I was there.

"Hey! What's going on?" He asked, smiling as he walked up to me.

"I broke up with him." A smile lit up my face as I said the words.

"Good for you. You don't need an asshole like that as a boyfriend." He looked straight into my eyes.

"Thanks for supporting me."

"Anytime. That's what I'm here for, but I do have to get back to work. I can't be out here too long." He waved his hands towards the line of carts. "They know how long it takes me to round these things up."

"I need to go too. I have to work tonight. I just wanted to let you know that I broke up with him." I shrugged.

"Well, bye." He turned to head back in to the store.

"Bye." I walked to my car and drove away.

I was a wreck as I drove home. I had broken up with Jay and while I was glad I did it; I was scared that he might be at my house waiting for me to get home. At the same time, I couldn't stop smiling whenever I thought about Paul.

He was such a nice guy and exceptionally supportive of me. I was beginning to like him. He helped me realize that what Jay was doing to me was not my fault and that I didn't deserve to be treated that way. He showed me that I had the courage to break up with Jay. Even if Paul and I remained just friends, he gave me hope that I wasn't completely worthless; that maybe there was a nice, good, respectful guy out there for me. It was just a glimmer of hope, but it was my lifeline.

Sooner than I realized I was pulling my car into my driveway. I was terrified that I might find Jay sitting with my mom, waiting for me. I hesitantly opened the door and peeked around, but he wasn't there, my mom was sitting alone in her usual spot on the couch surrounded by her bedding.

"What the hell did you do?" she screamed at me.

"What?" my hands flew protectively to cover my ears; her shrieking was painful.

"You broke up with Jay! He called me this morning before he left town and told me you gave him a letter and broke up with him." She shouted, still sitting on the couch.

"Yes! I did!" I stated through clenched teeth.

"Why in God's name would you do something that stupid?" my mom continued.

"It's not stupid!" I replied.

"I think it is. He thinks it is. He's willing to forgive you and forget the letter and get back together with you." She said this as though it were an actual option for me.

"I don't want to be with him anymore!"

"Why not? You'll never find someone like him to take care of you!" She was always his sales person.

"He hit me!" I admitted. "That's why I broke up with him." I thought that would end the conversation. "He hit me, okay?"

"What did you do to make him hit you?" I couldn't believe that those were the words she spoke after confessing to her that Jay had hit me.

"You think I did something to deserve getting hit? What happened to boys shouldn't hit girls? I didn't deserve to be hit! I can't do this!" I turned and walked out the door, past our car in the driveway and down the street. When I was a few houses away, I heard my mom yelling.

"Get back here! Mishell!" She was walking towards me, yelling. "You have no right to walk away from me when I'm talking to you!"

"I'm done talking to you!" I screamed. "You think I deserved to be hit! That I did something that made him hit me! Last night I had his hand print on my face! You think I did that?" Tears streamed down my cheeks as I remembered the sting of Jay striking me.

"Getting hit is no reason to break up with him. He just finished boot camp and is leaving again for his next training. He's probably all stressed out and then you probably said something that set him off. You can't blame him!" The words coming out of her mouth proved to me that she still didn't love me.

"Of course I can blame him! It was his handprint on my cheek! I didn't hit myself! I didn't grab his arm and fling his hand onto my face! I don't want to hear about it anymore! He hit me, I broke up with him! It's over!" I walked away from her again.

She followed me and placed a hand on my shoulder. "I just can't believe that you would throw away the last year and a half and all the promise of a future with him because he slapped you! That's ridiculous, Mishell!"

I turned on her, glaring at her. "Do you wanna know the real reason I broke up with him? Do you wanna hear the truth?" My mom just stood there on the sidewalk staring at me, hate streaming from her eyes. "He raped me! Is that what you want to hear? He forced me to have sex with him every time we were alone together. When you were in the shower in the hotel he raped me! Is that what you want to hear? I want it to stop! I never want that to happen again!"

Her eyes bored into me. Without an ounce of remorse in her voice, she patted me on the shoulder and said, "I hoped your first time would be better than that, but since you had sex with him you can't break up with him. In fact, you have to marry him now. Nobody else will want you!"

"I can't believe you!" I left her standing on the sidewalk. I ran back to our house, to my bedroom, slammed the door and collapsed onto my bed in a fit of tears. My brain could not, would not, process what she just said to me. That I had to marry the guy who raped me! No way! Her reaction cemented in my heart and mind that she honestly and truly did not love me the way a mother should love her children. I was worthless to her.

She came to my room. She spoke to me, quieter, but still icy. "I cannot believe that you would do this to me! What will people say about me as a mother when they find out that you're not a virgin? People will say I'm a bad mom and that I didn't train you right. You think having sex before marriage is acceptable. I can't believe you did this to me!"

I didn't say a word to her. I kept my face buried in my arms on my pillow, sobbing uncontrollably. She let out an exasperated sigh and walked out of my room.

My mom thought I did this to her. As if I asked to be raped. She would be perfectly happy for me to continue in that abusive relationship. She didn't care if I was happy, or safe, just that I didn't embarrass her by having sex before I got married.

She didn't get it; it wasn't about her! He raped me!

Chapter Eighteen

The next night that I closed at work was extremely slow, we completed all the cleaning tasks and inventory before ten, so we just waited around to lock the door. Just as I was turning the lock, a car pulled up. Not just any car though, it was a 1965 Mustang. I knew exactly who it was, and a smile spread across my face.

I waved and smiled at Paul as he turned off the engine. Even though I was fighting with my mom since breaking up with Jay, all that stress slipped away when I saw Paul. My coworker and I put the last few things away and clocked out. When Paul saw me walking to the door, he got out of his car and waited for me on the sidewalk.

I smiled as I walked up to him. "Hey!" I said.

"Hey! Want to sit with me for a while before you have to go home?"

"Of course." What else could I say? I wasn't in any rush to get home to my mom. I'd have stayed with him all night to stay away from house. We climbed into his Mustang and turned to face each other.

"So," Paul began. "You broke up with Jay."

"Yep." I nodded. "I got into a huge fight with my mom too. I haven't spoken to her for a few days now."

"I'm proud of you. I'm sure that wasn't easy for you." He smiled at me.

I looked down at my hands in my lap, "It wasn't easy, but I needed to do it." I looked into his eyes.

"Can I kiss you?" He asked.

I nodded and leaned towards him. "Yes."

He leaned in and kissed me so tenderly it took my breath away. It was filled with so much emotion; freedom, love, safety and value. He asked permission to kiss me, he didn't just do it. That's the right way to kiss someone. His hands weren't roaming over my body. I wasn't worried about him touching me in ways that made me uncomfortable. It was just a nice, sweet, honest kiss. Nothing more. I was loved again and I was happy.

I couldn't stay with him for too long, even though I didn't want to go home, I had to. My mom was waiting up for me when I walked in the door a few minutes later. I hadn't spoken to her since our fight on the sidewalk several days before. I had no intentions of talking to her that night either. I was done with her and trying to win her love and approval.

She started before I had even closed the door. "How long are you going to ignore me? I told your Aunt all about you and Jay having sex. Now she knows what kind of a girl you are."

I didn't hear what else she said, because I walked past her and retreated to the sanctuary and peace of my bedroom.

I fell asleep thinking about Paul that night and how much I appreciated the kind of person he was; kind, supportive, helpful, respectful and so many other things that Jay had not been and my parents were not. The one thing about Paul that was hard for me was the fact that he wasn't a Christian. That didn't make me think any less of him, it made me question God and all I had been taught about relationships when I was younger.

Jay was a Christian and according to what I had learned in church and from my mom, that was the top priority when looking for a boyfriend or future husband. If they were not a Christian, then they were flawed and unfit for a relationship with a believer. There was a verse that was forever quoted; 2 Corinthians 6:14 "Do not be yoked together with unbelievers. For what do righteousness and wickedness have in common? Or what fellowship can light have with darkness?" I knew the verse by heart. I had been taught what it meant about relationships, including friendships, by my mom since I was eight years old.

That verse meant that no Christian should ever be in any sort of relationship with someone who did not believe in God. Period. End of discussion. They would never measure up, they could not be trusted, they had no morals they were straight from the devil. A Christian would be destroyed by them and end up in hell with them.

Life was showing me that wasn't always the truth. First, there was Jay. From the very beginning of the relationship, that night I met him and we parked on a dark country road, at his request, he constantly pressured me to go farther sexually than I wanted to. He dismissed me when I would tell him no, then he raped me. Not just once, but continually over several months.

Next, there was my mom. She taught me that sex before marriage was a sin and I would have to plead for God's forgiveness if I ever did have sex. Also, it was up to me, as a girl, to guard my virginity and make sure that I never gave it up to anybody except my husband. When I told her what happened with Jay, what he did to me, she didn't care! She told me that it was my duty as a Christian to marry him since I had sex with him. If I didn't marry him, I was going to hell because I had sex with someone other than my husband. I simply couldn't believe that God would want me to marry a man that raped me and made me feel so terribly unloved and worthless.

Finally, there was Paul. He wasn't a Christian, but he was everything that Jay wasn't. He cared about me and others. He was supportive and respectful. He was everything that a young girl would want in a boyfriend. When I had met Jay, I wanted so much to be loved that I put up with his crap. I didn't have to do that with Paul. He was the one who helped me put into words how I felt about Jay and what he did to me. He encouraged me when I needed it to stand up to

Jay and break up with him. How was I supposed to believe that Jay was God's plan for my life and Paul wasn't when Paul was a much better human being?

I was completely and utterly confused. Maybe God didn't have a grand plan for my life. Maybe my mom was wrong about how involved God was in our relationships. Maybe God could love me no matter who I dated. Maybe God would despise me no matter who I dated. It wasn't like I felt a whole lot of God's presence when I was with Jay. So, did it matter to God who I dated?

I didn't want to give up on God completely. I knew he existed. I couldn't look around at the beauty of creation and not believe that there was a supreme being that created it all. I couldn't believe that people just happened over billions of years of evolution. With how amazing and complex humans are I could only believe that we were lovingly created by our Maker, God.

If God existed though, why did bad things happen, especially to good people? Why was I put into a family that didn't value me? I couldn't have done something bad before I was born to deserve the parents I had. And why, when I was trying to do what I believed God wanted, by dating a Christian, did I get broken down, verbally abused, sexually abused and raped? Did God think I deserved those things? I didn't think I deserved those things and I couldn't believe that God thought that either.

I struggled to come to a resolution. I liked Paul. He was a very good person and it didn't matter to me if he was a Christian or not, he was a better person than Jay or either of my parents were. God could judge me however He wanted to for that decision.

Chapter Nineteen

I spent as much time with Paul as I possibly could and I started speaking to my mom again. I did all the grocery shopping and took Stefyni and Keeth to any appointments they may have had, which forced me to talk to her to make all those arrangements. I still refused to talk about Jay or Paul with her, even though she continuously brought Jay up and informed me that that I needed to ask him to take me back. When she wasn't trying to play matchmaker for Jay, she was demeaning me and my choice to date Paul. She never missed an opportunity to remind me that I was going straight to hell because I was dating an unbeliever.

Even though I had to communicate with her about my driving duties, I didn't respond to a lot she had to say to me. Somehow, I found the strength to tell her that I would not be doing the driving duties and grocery shopping if I was not allowed to use the car in my free time to go where I wanted. I refused to have responsibilities anymore without some privileges too. She conceded as long as I promised to let her know where I planned to be or what I planned to do.

Paul asked me to go to my junior prom with him. I was thrilled to be going with him, but I was not looking forward to telling my mom about the date. For one thing, I would need a later curfew since the dance wouldn't be over until midnight and that was my curfew. Secondly, I thought that it was her responsibility, as my mom, to buy my dress, since I didn't get any allowance. I dreaded the conversation and decided to get it over with sooner rather than later.

I approached my mom carefully one day after school. I waited until a commercial came on because she hated when we interrupted her shows. I sat on the couch opposite of her so we were sitting face to face. I took a deep, calming breath before beginning, "Ma? Can I talk to you?"

She took a drag off her cigarette, held her breath for a moment and blew the smoke directly at me. "Has hell frozen over and the devil skated away? You want to talk to me? I don't have to come beg you to talk to me? What do you want?"

I exhaled and held my breath, waiting for the smoke to clear before starting. "I've decided to go to my prom with Paul." The words fell over each other as I spoke them.

"What about Jay?" She always had to steer the conversation to him.

"I broke up with him. I'm dating Paul now and I want to go to my prom with him." I was doing my best to stay calm and have patience.

"Jay told me that he'd take leave for a weekend to take you to your prom." She continued as if I hadn't just spoken.

I ignored her too and continued. "I'd really appreciate it if you would buy my dress and go shopping with me." I didn't want to go shopping with her, but if it convinced her to buy my dress, I would certainly suffer it.

She exhaled another puff of smoke in my face. "So you're talking to me to try to get me to buy you a prom dress." Another drag, another exhale. "Tell you what, I'll buy your prom dress, but you have to go to the prom with Jay."

Was she being serious? I would not be going to my prom with an abusing rapist! I held my tongue. It was excruciating. "I'm going with Paul. I'll buy my own dress and I'll be home by one in the morning."

"Your curfew is midnight." Another cloud of smoke blown my way.

"I know, but prom doesn't even get over until midnight, so I'll be home by one." My voice sounded much calmer than I felt. I wanted to yell at her to stop blowing smoke my way, to leave me alone about Jay, to accept the fact that I was dating Paul and I would not be going to hell for it.

"You're obviously going to do whatever you want to anyway." She turned away from me and back to the television, dismissing me once again.

Sometime after that enlightening and oh-so-productive conversation with my mom, I went shopping for a prom dress. Did I mention that I hate shopping? Especially for dresses, but I was looking forward to prom and I wanted to be cute. A few hours after arriving at the mall I had succeeded in buying the perfect dress for my junior prom. It was a strapless, knee length formal dress. The body was light pink with a sweetheart neckline and the skirt was three layers of light pink and white stripes with tulle underneath for bounce. It was absolutely adorable and it looked amazing on me. I used my savings to buy it and I was proud of myself.

When I got home I didn't want to take the dress inside because cigarette smell would infiltrate every fiber, but I had to keep it somewhere until prom. I tied the plastic bag closed and walked through the house as fast as I could to hang it in my closet, hoping it was fast enough to keep the cigarette stench out of my dress.

As soon as I shut my closet door after hanging up the dress, the telephone rang.

I heard my mom say, "Hello." Then she spoke loud enough for me to hear "Mishell, it's for you!"

Something was off in the way she sounded. She had a lilt in her voice as if she was smiling when she called me to the phone. If it was Paul, her voice would have been dripping with disdain. If it was someone she didn't know, she would sound indifferent. I was breathing rapidly as I walked down the hallway. My hand shook as I took the receiver from her hand. I knew who it was before I even said hello.

"Hey, Mitch!"

My skin crawled at the sound of his voice. I didn't respond, I was frozen.

"I heard you went shopping today." He accused.

My mom, the snitch. "Yes." Flat.

"That's good because I just got the weekend of your prom approved for leave and I'll be there to take you." As though he was giving me the best news in the world.

"No!" I spat. "I'm not going with you. I'm going with Paul." My voice sounded more firm and decisive than I felt; my voice wasn't shaking as bad as my hand. He frightened me, even over the phone. I decided to end the conversation, rather than argue, and hung up on him.

I couldn't believe what my mom had done! How low would she go? She let Jay know when prom would be and that I had gone shopping that day! She was sabotaging my life! I wanted to turn on her, to scream and yell at her, but I realized that wouldn't change anything. She wouldn't stop until I did what she wanted. I would never break up with Paul and get back together with Jay!

I stomped back to my room, without saying a word to her. I wouldn't even bother trying with her. She obviously didn't care about me or what I wanted, so what was the point?

Paul was definitely a source of the newfound strength and resolve I had. He and his family liked me. Sometimes they let me hang out at their house when Paul was at work or school, just so I wouldn't have to be at home. I felt like I had finally found a family, a place to belong and call home. I was valued not by just one person, but a whole family.

Time passed by slowly as I waited for prom. When it finally arrived, I spent most of the day at home preparing myself. I couldn't afford to get my hair and makeup done, so I did it all myself. I did my best to remain in my bedroom and away from my mom's cigarette smell; I didn't want that stench permeating my hair and skin before prom.

Paul picked me up in his Mustang and drove us to dinner at an Italian restaurant. I was nervous because I didn't want to get spaghetti sauce on my dress. Eventually, I relaxed and enjoyed dinner. After dinner, we went to the prom. When we walked in we received our prom favors, a pocket mirror in a plastic case with the prom date on it. Kind of cheesy, but I didn't care, I was at Prom with an incredible date. We took pictures, then went down to the dance floor. We didn't stay long, we had other plans for the night.

Paul and I had met cruising and many of our date nights involved cruising in his Mustang for a few hours. It was a lot of fun driving up and down the same street with the music blaring. Unfortunately, prom night was the last night for cruising because the city had passed an ordinance making cruising illegal because of the problems it supposedly caused. According to police there was increased gang activity, more drugs and too many fights happening during the cruises.

So, after spending a little bit of time at the prom we planned on enjoying the last night to legally cruise. We left the prom, which was being held at an arena at one end of the cruise strip. Before we left the parking lot, I encouraged Paul to remove the garter belt I was wearing just above the hem of my dress and hang it on his rearview mirror. I appreciated that there was no pressure to do more.

The night of my Junior Prom was amazing, I'll never forget it, and I was home by one in the morning which was exactly when I told my mom to expect me. She wasn't awake when I got in, so I quietly made my way to my room, changed out of my prom dress into pajamas, crawled into bed and went to sleep; exhausted and exhilarated.

When I awoke in the morning I smiled at the memory of the night before. Paul had not forced me to have sex with him, it wasn't even an expectation for him, even though it was Prom night and so many other guys expected it. Paul was a complete gentleman, he never pressured me beyond what I was comfortable with. His patience allowed me to be extremely comfortable with him. It had been an amazing, comfortable night.

I wasn't looking forward to going to church that morning. I would have preferred staying in bed, reflecting on my night with Paul. I didn't want to hear about how much God was upset with me for having premarital sex or that I was going to hell for dating a non-Christian. I had changed churches since I broke up with Jay, but the message was still the same; perfection was the expectation if you wanted to get into Heaven.

Chapter Twenty

The phone rang. I answered it, "Hello!"

"Hey, Mitch!" It was Jay. "I came all the way from San Diego and you went to prom with some other guy!"

"I told you I was." I forced my voice to remain calm, even though I wasn't.

"Want to know what I've learned in the Marines? I learned how to kill a guy in three moves. That's what I want to do to the guy you went out with. Tell me where he lives!"

"No." I shuddered at the thought of what he just said.

"I'll find out and when I do he'll regret ever dating you." He threatened.

In my mind, I said "like I regret dating you." The words that actually came out of my mouth were, "I don't want you to hurt him. Please don't." I pleaded.

"Come talk to me then. If you come over and break up with me face to face, I'll leave you alone and I won't hurt him. If you can look me in the eyes and tell me you don't love me, I'll be done with you. I'll never bother you again."

"I just have to tell you I don't love you?" I questioned, doubting him.

"Yes." He replied.

"And you won't hurt me or Paul?" I knew what he was capable of and didn't trust him.

"Correct." He answered with an icy calm.

My mom had left her spot on the couch to stand beside me and listen to the conversation. "Is that Jay? I told him that you were seeing somebody else." She sounded like a child who had tattled on me to the teacher. "You need to go talk to him. Straighten this all out."

"I'll be there in a few minutes." I hung up on him. I was scared to see him, but if it meant he would finally leave me alone I had to try.

"Ma, I'm going to Jay's."

"Finally. I'm glad you've come to your senses." She gave me a hug. I didn't hug her back. "Take as long as you need. Don't screw this up."

I knew she was hoping that I'd get back together with Jay, but there was no way I would ever do that. I would not continue to date the person who raped me!

On the drive to Jay's house my heart raced, my breathing was shallow and quick, my palms were sweating. I almost drove straight to Paul's house instead. The only reason I didn't was because I was scared that Jay would find him and try to kill him or me. I had to have the courage to stop Jay from controlling my life and my emotions. I needed to end the control he had over me once and for all.

I could see Jay standing in his driveway as I turned the corner onto his street. He looked irate. I parked near the curb and walked up to him. "All I have to do is tell you I don't love you, right?" I started talking before I could chicken out and leave without ending this.

"Yes, look me in the eye and tell me you don't love me and I won't kill this other guy."

I looked up into his deep brown eyes, wondering how I didn't see the kind of person he was from the beginning. "I don't love you." It was flat and emotionless.

"I don't believe you!" he snapped. Before I knew it, he had grabbed my arm and was dragging me towards his house. He pulled me inside and I realized that either nobody was home or they were hiding. I was alone with a turbulent Jay, who only minutes before informed me that he could kill a guy in three moves.

He pulled me down the hall to his bedroom. I twisted my arm trying to free myself from his grip. When we got to the doorway of his room I grasped the door jamb, holding on as tight as I could. He was too strong for me and easily pulled me into his room. He closed and locked the door and threw me down onto the bed.

I tried to get away, but he was faster than I was. He pinned me on the mattress, against the wall with one arm while taking his shorts off with the other. I continued struggling against him until he reached into my shorts and moved my panties aside. Once again he raped me. The words flashed through my mind like a credits list at the end of a movie.

Slut.
Whore.
Cheater.
Unlovable.
Damaged.
Used.
Worthless.

I laid there, unmoving, defeated and crying until he finished and let me up.

"You can clean up and leave. I have to get back to San Diego. I'm done with you." He said as he rolled over on his bed.

I left in tears. I didn't want to go home, but I didn't want to go to Paul's either. I was too ashamed to let Paul know that I had let Jay rape me again, so I just drove.

Jay had absolutely, utterly, destroyed me. He had taken, by force, what I had been taught was the most precious gift I had to give; my virginity. He stole my feeling of security. He had thrown away what little identity I had of myself so that all I knew was his version of me, but I had spent the past few months learning who I was without Jay and without my mom. I liked the person that I was becoming. I didn't like what Jay just did to me.

After seeing that movie with Shauna, Paul and Tom, I knew that Jay didn't love me. He loved controlling and abusing me, just like the husband in the movie only loved to control and abuse his wife. That movie opened my eyes to so many things. It gave me words to go along with the feelings I had been experiencing. It showed me that I don't have to put up with abuse of any kind, by anybody, for any reason.

I wasn't a bad person and didn't deserve what Jay did to me, but it was difficult to convince my heart of that. I had been conditioned to believe that God takes care of those He is happy with and He punished those who sinned. I couldn't figure out what I had done to deserve being raped by Jay and unloved by my mom. I had always loved God and always tried to do what I thought would make Him happy. I went to church as often as I could. I slept with the Bible beside my pillow and read it often, most of my friends were Christians and I did my best to honor my parents, even when I didn't feel like they deserved it. I talked to people about Jesus and did my absolute best to be as perfect as God wanted me to be.

Where did that get me?

Raped.

Used.

Broken.

That's where being good had gotten me.

I didn't have a family that loved me, took care of me or valued me. Instead I had a dad whose advice was not to have sex with every Tom, Dick and Harry; if they tried to force me, I should kick them in the balls and run. (Maybe if I had done what he suggested, things wouldn't have gotten so bad with Jay.) My mom could barely take care of herself, let alone three teenaged kids. She was sick so often by this point that she didn't even work any longer.

I was only sixteen years old, but I felt so much older. I was a kid with adult responsibilities and I hated it. I wanted to be a normal teenager, able to hang out with friends and not worry about how I was going to fit in homework, finding a new job, taking my brother and sister to all their appointments and school as well as do the grocery shopping and get my mom and grandma to all their doctor's appointments. It was overwhelming.

My parents were only happy with me when I did what they wanted. So, I worked hard, hoping I could make them love me again. That's what I carried into my relationship with Jay; that I had to earn his love and acceptance. I allowed him to do things to me that I never wanted to do, just to keep him happy.

Then I met Paul. I don't know if things changed because of Paul or because of the movie we saw on our first date, or because Jay had been gone, but I knew I was changing. I was a valuable human being. It was possible for people to accept and love me without having to compromise who I was. I liked who I was becoming and what I was learning about love and acceptance.

Chapter Twenty-One

The end of my junior year of high school was approaching and I had a lot of things to do before the last day arrived. One of which was that I had to pass all my classes. While most of them were no problem, I was struggling with Algebra II. Adding letters to numbers wasn't working out in my brain too well. It was hard on me to not do well in a class, because I had always excelled in school. Paul helped me through the end of Algebra II and I ended up earning a 'D,' passing, but not well enough for college. It was the hardest I had ever worked in a class and the lowest grade I had ever received.

Picking classes for my senior year was another chore. I had to take Chemistry, because I needed another science class to graduate. I also wanted to take Algebra II again to improve my grade for college. All seniors had to take Government and Economics, so there was another one I signed up for. I also had to take my second year of French which left me with two periods that I could choose elective classes for.

My plan was to be out of my house as soon as possible after graduation and having a good job would help make that happen. I wanted to eventually become a nurse, because it would make my mom proud of me, but I didn't want to wait that long to get a decent paying job.

Our school district had a program, which allowed students to earn entry level certificates in various industries. One of them was a certified nursing assistant, CNA, program. As a CNA, I would be able to get a job in a hospital or doctor's office as early as the following summer. I could learn about the industry I wanted to eventually be in and be able to earn money right out of high school. The faster I earned money, the faster I would be able to escape my mom so of course, I signed up for that class. It met two hours a day. Mondays and Fridays would be classroom days and Tuesday through Thursday would be clinical hours where we trained in a convalescent hospital.

I was so excited to tell my mom about me training to be a nurse, I raced home to tell her about the program. I expected her to be proud of me since I was following in her footsteps and going into nursing.

As soon as I walked in the door, I sat on the couch across from her. "Ma, guess what I did today?"

She drew her eyes away from the television to look at me as she responded. "Broke up with Paul and got back together with Jay."

"Not gonna happen." I replied without skipping a beat. "I signed up for a CNA class for next year. I'll be able to get certified and get a job by next summer!"

"I thought you wanted to be a registered nurse." She stated.

"I do. That's why I signed up for the class. I can start learning nursing stuff now. I don't have to wait until college. Then when I'm in college I'll have a job." I was very proud of myself.

"You know what a nursing assistant does don't you?" she asked condescendingly.

"Yes. They take temperatures, blood pressure and pulses, they help the nurses." I answered confidently.

"Actually, all a nurse's assistant gets to do is clean up the messes that people make in their beds when they vomit, pee or poop themselves. They have to give bed baths to nasty, dirty people and empty catheters, you know, pee bags." She seemed to delight in belittling me.

"I thought you'd be proud of me for doing this! I'll be learning to be a nurse!" I was on the verge of tears.

"When you become an actual nurse, then, I'll be proud of you." To signify she was done with me, she turned back to the television and lit another cigarette.

I walked to my room in defeat, I would never be good enough for her. All she cared about was what I could do for her; fix meals, go shopping, run errands, take her to the doctor, clean the house. She didn't want children, she wanted servants to be at her beck and call and I was done doing that. I would continue to do what I needed to help Stef and Keeth, but I was done trying to please my mom.

Chapter Twenty-Two

The end of my junior year had finally arrived. Unlike the past two summers, I was waiting anxiously for the final bell to ring. The bell that would usher in days and days of freedom. I had two months off school, my brother would be at my dad's most days and Stefyni had a job. I had virtually no responsibilities beyond grocery shopping. I planned on spending as much time as possible away from my house and with Paul.

The day I truly felt accepted by Paul's family was his nineteenth birthday. They had a family get together to celebrate and they included me, I was the only non-relative in attendance. I finally had a safe place to be, a place to call home. This family loved and accepted me, even with my past, knowing that I had been raped.

As the lazy days of summer passed, Paul taught me how to ride jet skis. His family had property and a boat launch on the river. Being near the water almost daily was rejuvenating. It seemed the water, sun and of course companionship was healing my heart. I was at peace with myself when I was with Paul and his family.

On the other hand, when I was with my mom there was constant turmoil and strife. She constantly criticized me and my choice to date Paul. She never missed an opportunity to let me know that I was going straight to hell because I was "unequally yoked with an unbeliever."

Besides giving me a hard time about Paul, my mom loved telling me what a horrible daughter I was turning out to be. Her conversations to me were always about me hating her and our family or letting me know that I wasn't taking care of my duties of cleaning the house for her, taking care of my siblings and making dinner.

All her nagging did was make me ask for more hours at work and spend more time at Paul's house with him and his family. I often worked the lunch shift and then I'd head to Paul's house to wait until he got out of class or off of work. Then we'd hang out watching movies or go jet skiing on the river. It was so good to finally belong somewhere without always having to prove myself. I was relaxed. I was home.

My mom must have sensed she was losing me because she stepped up her game. Up to that point she had only been harassing me at home, but she began to harass me wherever I went. When I went to a friend's house, I had to give her their phone number, so she could call and make sure I was where I said I'd be. I had made a few new friends while dating Paul. Most of them were people I knew from school, but was hanging out with them more now. My mom didn't trust that I could have friends other than Shauna and Dustin, since those were the only two friends I had been allowed to have while I dated Jay. I was tired of her spying on me.

For the Fourth of July, Paul and I had plans to spend the day with some friends and then I was going to spend the night with one of them. I gave my mom her phone number and let her know that we'd be back there sometime after the fireworks. I didn't think there would be any problems, it was going to be a great day.

We started out the morning jet skiing and relaxing at the river. After lunch, we met up with the friends and went back to the river. As the afternoon wore on, more and more of Paul's family began to arrive, by evening we were all gathered along the water's edge enjoying a big dinner. It was by far shaping up to be the best Fourth of July I had ever experienced.

One of Paul's family members had a boat and after dinner we piled as many people as we could into it and enjoyed an evening cruise along the river. We cruised past the little lake the city had built where you could see families enjoying their time on the beach. The water lapped quietly along the riverbank as we cruised along. The trees along the banks were green and lush and cast just enough shade to break the heat of the day. I was snuggled under Paul's arm, completely happy and enjoying the peaceful evening on the water. I had no idea that such a beautiful, enchanting place existed in our little town.

Dusk brought with it the promise of fireworks, so I once again climbed into a boat with Paul and a few others. We slowly navigated the river, until we came to an incredible spot to watch the fireworks right below where they would be exploding in the cool night sky. Paul moved to sit on the bottom of the boat with his back against the side and his legs stretched out in front of him. I sat between his legs, leaning back against his chest, his arms wrapped around me.

When the fireworks began, I snuggled back into Paul's chest. He held me tighter as we both looked up to the sky. The fireworks were exploding just above us, lighting up the sky in amazing colors of red, white, blue, yellow, green, and purple. It was one of the most beautiful fireworks shows I had ever seen, and I was enjoying them with someone who loved and respected me.

When the grand finale concluded the fireworks show, we slowly made our way back to the dock. The sound of the water lapping at the side of the boat was intoxicating, I never wanted the evening to end, but I was supposed to spend the night at my friend's house. However, she had made plans to stay the night with the guy she was with so the four of us made our way to his house. The two of them went and did their thing, while Paul and I did ours. I drank my very first wine cooler and ended up falling asleep in Paul's arms.

When I drove home the next morning it seemed like my life was on the right track. I was doing what I wanted instead of allowing others to control me. I was free, unlike I had ever been before. It was a perfect ending to an

Independence Day celebration because that is what I finally felt; independent.

When I walked in the front door that morning, my mom was in her usual spot on the end of the couch facing the door, her bedding stacked neatly next to her. She had her feet tucked underneath her, leaning on the armrest as though it was holding her up, a cigarette between her fingers.

I barely had the door closed when she attacked. "Where have you been?"

"You know I stayed the night with Jennifer." I responded.

"That's what you told me! I called her house last night and her mom said she was staying the night with you!" She spat before taking a deep pull from her cigarette and blowing the smoke towards me.

"You think I'm lying to you? I was with Jennifer!" In a few moments, I had gone from being a valuable human being, making my own way to worthless daughter.

"Then why did her mom say she was staying with you?" She glared.

"We didn't stay at her house though." Mumbling, no matter how much she yelled, I couldn't lie to my mom.

"You were at Paul's, weren't you?" She shook her head in disgust.

"No, we didn't stay at Paul's either." I whispered.

"Where were you? I was worried all night! I had no idea where you were?" Her eyes bored into me.

"We stayed at another guy's house." I looked down at the strands of tan carpet around my feet.

"We who?" She sounded stern.

"Jennifer and I." I continued to look at the floor, searching for stains, trash or anything else that would take my attention away from my mom's eyes trying to see through me.

"Who else was there, Mishell?" she continued, trying to get the whole truth from me.

"Jennifer, the guy and me."

"Paul wasn't there?" She knew I wasn't telling her everything.

"Yes. He was there too." I admitted. I could keep things from her, but when confronted I was unable or unwilling to lie to her.

"You stayed the night with Paul?" Each word was full of disappointment that I had stayed the night with Paul.

"And Jennifer." I wanted her to know I wasn't alone with Paul. "And the guy whose house we were at."

"Were his parents there? Do you even know his name?"

"No, I don't remember his name and his parents weren't there." I hated telling her this, but no matter how she'd judge me, I couldn't lie to her. I wanted her to know who I was and the choices I made and love me any way.

"So you two girls stayed the night with two boys! Did I raise you to sleep with whoever you want, whenever you want? You already had sex with Jay! He should be the one you're with, not Paul. You know you're going straight to hell for the way you're behaving and the choices you're making! I hope you're happy, because nobody else is." Her voice rose with each word, until it was a shrill storm, ripping me to pieces.

Without responding to her again, I walked down the hall to my room. I grabbed clean clothes and stomped to the bathroom to shower. The warm water hit my face and mixed with the salty tears coursing down my cheeks. There was no way my mom would ever love me if I continued making my own choices about my relationships with boys and with God. She believed that since I was dating a non-Christian that I was bound for hell and that she needed to remind me of that nonstop to get me back to following the Lord. All it was doing was pushing me farther away from her.

    I refused to stay home that morning and listen to my mom tell me what a horrible person I was or get me down by reminding me over and over that I was going to hell for the choices I was making. I wouldn't allow her to control me anymore. I had a person who loved me and treated me with respect. His family welcomed and accepted me. I finally had a place to belong and that's where I was going to spend my day; with people who cared about me as a person.

    At my house, I had no control of my own life. I wasn't allowed to be who I was and make my own decisions. I had to be quiet and acquiesce to my mom's demands or suffer her wrath, which was getting to be more turbulent by the day.

    After my shower, I stayed in my room until I calmed down enough to face my mom on my way out of the house. As I walked towards the front door she was still sitting in the same spot on the couch, bathrobe wrapped around her, pillows and blankets piled next to her and a cigarette between her fingers. As I neared the door, she took a drag from the cigarette before smashing it in the ashtray on the table beside her, I thought I was going to get away without another word from her, but she turned on me.

    "You probably think I'm done talking to you about what you did last night." Her lips curled as she spoke, as though my very presence repulsed her.

    "There's always hope." I replied, my words dripping with sarcasm.

    She lit another cigarette. "You know; I don't even think you're a Christian anymore. How can you be when you lie, sleep with boys that you aren't married to and treat me so badly?" She put the cigarette to her lips and inhaled deeply.

    I just stared at her. It was the same conversation with her all the time. I did the things that needed to be done, like driving people to appointments and grocery shopping, helped with cleaning the house and drove Stefyni and I to youth group. I definitely wasn't perfect and I never would be.

Her voice softened, just a little, the edge was gone. "You were raised better than this, Mishell. You know God isn't happy with you right now. You're dating someone who is not a Christian. You don't have any respect for me. You run around and do whatever you want. You lied to me about where you were staying last night, just to spend the night with Paul."

"I didn't lie on purpose. I was planning to stay at Jennifer's. Then Paul invited this guy to the Fourth of July and Jennifer liked him. She wanted to spend the night with him so she called her mom and told her she was staying at my house. I went along with it and I didn't want to be alone while she was messing around with him, so Paul stayed too."

"You could've come home instead of going with her." She had a solution for everything.

"I wasn't going to leave her alone with a boy she just met yesterday!" Didn't she know the friend code?

"You could've called." She continued.

"At eleven o'clock? You'd be asleep or mad that I called. It doesn't matter what I do, it's always the wrong choice. You're always yelling at me! I can't do anything good enough for you!" It felt good to finally be getting this off my chest and let her know what was on my mind.

"That's not true. You are such a different person now than when you were dating Jay. You used to care about me and you always did what I needed you to do. Now you are so selfish!" She tore her slipper from her foot and threw it towards me. It landed with a thump at my feet.

"I'm not being selfish; I'm living my life instead of letting other people tell me what to do!" I stormed out the door. I was done listening to her tell me how much better things had been for her when I was dating Jay. He controlled me and told me what to do, how to act and who I could have as friends. She was trying to take his place in controlling me. I refused to be controlled, I just wanted to be loved and accepted. Was that too much to hope for from my own family?

Chapter Twenty-Three

A few weeks later I celebrated my seventeenth birthday with Paul. He picked me up in the morning and we drove to Santa Cruz, to spend the day at the Boardwalk. We planned to spend the day together riding roller coasters, eating and just having fun.

As we drove to Santa Cruz, I was amazed at how comfortable it was to be with Paul. The stress of my mom and my life at home just melted away when I was with him. It felt so good to not be tense and ready to fight or flee at any second. I was relaxed and enjoying things. I didn't have to worry about what my mom would say next, or how bad she would make me feel, because she wasn't there. I was one-hundred percent, entirely, enveloped in the moment with Paul. Nothing from my past was getting in the way and the only future I wanted was with him.

When we finally arrived in Santa Cruz, after a two and half hour drive, we found parking on a side street near the Boardwalk. We walked from there to the beach and Boardwalk. It wasn't far considering we'd be walking all day.

We walked hand in hand from ride to ride. Talking, laughing, joking and planning. I knew I was in love. I had found a person who loved and accepted me with all my flaws and imperfections. He knew about Jay; he knew about my mom and he still chose me. He was patient in helping me deal with and heal from what Jay did to me. He knew me, who I really was. I could look into his eyes and know he cared and that he wanted to know everything there was to know about me.

That day, like so many times before, the conversation turned to my childhood and how I'd never been allowed to be a kid. My mom had allowed me to play on a softball team for a few years, but at the same time I was expected to take care of Stefyni and Keeth. I made sure we ate by making all our meals. By the time I was eight years old, I could microwave almost anything, knew how to make tacos, complete with fried corn tortillas, top ramen and pancakes, and I could fry eggs, or boil them, if that's what we wanted. My sister, Cindy, helped a lot in teaching me how to do all that, but she was in high school and didn't spend a lot of time at home.

However, she did spend time at home when she had parties. She and my mom both liked to throw parties. Together. Thirty something parents partying with teenagers and I was the lucky one who got to watch the children of my mom's friends while they partied. Usually only a couple of other kids showed up, but it was up to me to make sure we all stayed away from the beer and other drinks. They also smoked at the parties, sometimes cigarettes, since that was my mom's absolute favorite thing to do, but they also smoked marijuana.

At one of the parties my brother found the keg and drank straight from the tap. Then he ran up and down the hallway screaming it was gross. Then he went straight back to the keg and did it again. I thought it was pretty funny, the party guests thought it was hilarious. I finally got him to stop and got him back to our bedroom, but not before my mom yelled at me for allowing him to do that.

Even at eight years old, I knew that it shouldn't have been up to me to keep brother out of trouble. My mom shouldn't have been having parties with my teenage sister and her friends and leaving me to take care of the kids. She should have been teaching us the dangers of drinking instead of indulging in drinking or growing her own marijuana in the backyard.

Now at seventeen years old, I just wanted to be a normal teenager. I didn't want to worry about what to cook for dinner or who had to get where by when. I wanted to do homework and think about college and what I was going to do with my life. I wanted to hang out with my friends. I didn't want to work anymore to earn my mom's love. I just wanted her to love me for who I was, instead of only loving me when I was her version of who I should be. I should have been able to be myself and have my mom love me, but I was realizing that wasn't how it was working out to be.

That realization hurt. Especially on my birthday. She did absolutely nothing to help me celebrate. She gave birth to me, you'd think there'd be some love there, but I got nothing from her. Maybe she wanted a bravo for bringing me into the world, I don't know.

I do know that I was having one of my best birthdays ever. I had thought that my fifteenth birthday with Jay was nice, but I was so nervous that day. I couldn't relax and be myself because I was so busy trying to behave in a way that would guarantee that he'd like me. I didn't feel that way with Paul. I could relax and just be me because I was secure in how Paul felt about me.

I was completely enjoying the day. The rides were fun, but the conversation with Paul was what made the day amazing. We could talk about anything and everything. Unfortunately, the day eventually had to end so we walked back to his car. We were still about a block away when we noticed something in the windshield wiper. When we got to the car we saw that it was a parking ticket. I guess we chose the wrong place to park.

A few days later Paul and I were together again, as we were most days. Paul started the conversation. "I talked to my parents about you and your mom. They're willing to get guardianship of you so you don't have to be there anymore."

"I can't just leave her. She's my mom. I mean I plan on leaving as soon as I turn eighteen, but not yet." I had been dreaming of the day I could escape my family, but this was sudden.

"You can stay in the extra room and you won't have to worry about anything anymore. You can be a part of our family. Your mom doesn't take care of you." His voice gave away his concern for me.

"That'd leave Stef and Keeth alone with her. I don't think I can do that. Maybe when Stef can drive. Then she can do all the errands for my mom." I didn't want to leave them to fend for themselves, at least with me there, she took it all out on me.

"You don't owe your mom anything. She hasn't taken care of you your whole life. You have all the responsibility of an adult and you're only seventeen. You deserve to be a kid for a little bit. You've never been able to just be a kid."

"That's true, but it would hurt my mom. I don't want to hurt her feelings." I knew she didn't care about me, but I didn't want to hurt her. Deep down I still wanted her to love me. If I left, I knew I'd never have the chance to make her love me. I also wanted to follow the commandment to honor your parents.

"And she doesn't hurt you? She doesn't even care about you except what you can do for her." He was repeating things I'd told him. It was strange hearing it from someone else.

"You're right again, Paul. I know it doesn't make sense, but I don't want to hurt her." Or upset God, I added to myself.

"Can we just talk to my parents about it please? You can see what they have to say and then make a decision. It's not like it's gonna happen overnight. There's paperwork to do and that'll take time."

"Alright. Let's talk to your parents." I conceded. The idea was tempting, I already felt at home with his family. Talking to them couldn't hurt, right?

By the time I talked to them, I was already warming up to the idea of not living with my mom any longer. All she and I did anymore was fight. She wasn't happy that I was becoming my own person and not allowing myself to be at her beck and call any longer. I did what needed to be done and that was it, groceries and doctor's appointments; nothing more. When I was home though all she did was tell me what a horrible daughter I was and that I was going to hell for the way I was living my life.

The guidelines for me to live with them seemed doable. I would have the spare bedroom, right next to theirs. I would have to help with chores and keep up in school. I was totally capable of doing those things.

What I wasn't prepared to do was to stop going to church. If I moved in with them I wouldn't have my car, since it belonged to my mom. I couldn't quite say, "Hey mom, I'm moving in with this other family and I'm taking your car with me." Paul didn't go to church with me and it was about a thirty-minute drive from his house, so I wouldn't have a way to get to church.

Even though I was not doing what my mom wanted me to do, being the "perfect" Christian, God was still important to me. I often questioned where He was in my life, but I wanted God in my life. I was beginning to believe that God could love me, even if I wasn't perfect, even when I made mistakes, and even if my mom didn't love me. I still attended youth group and Sunday services with Stefyni because I enjoyed the music and learning about God.

Another thing I wasn't prepared to do was to leave my siblings alone with my mom. She wasn't able to drive anymore because of being dizzy most of the time and Stefyni didn't have her driver's license yet. Keeth was still in junior high, he couldn't do much to help with anything besides keeping the house clean. At least Stefyni could cook. My grandma lived with us too, she helped with laundry and cooking recently, but she had never learned to drive. If I moved out it would leave the entire family without a driver.

Cindy lived nearby and could help, but she was finishing college and had a baby.

Was any of that even my responsibility though? I mean, shouldn't my mom have been taking care of us, not us taking care of her? I shouldn't have to take my little brother and sister to their orthodontist appointments. I shouldn't have to take my mom to doctor appointments. I shouldn't have to do the grocery shopping.

I decided to move in with Paul's family. Between how they accepted me and what I was learning about God at church, I was starting to think that maybe, just maybe, I wasn't as worthless as I felt. Maybe I was lovable, capable and important. Maybe I could be loved and accepted for just being me.

A few weeks later, Paul's parents gave me a form they had written to become my guardians. I needed to get my mom to sign it, and get it back to them. It was the beginning of a new chapter in my life. I went home that day, walked through the front door and found my mom in her usual place, sitting at the end of the couch opposite the door, legs tucked beneath her, cigarette in hand.

"So, you've decided to grace us with your presence today." She said when I sat down at the edge of the couch as far away from her as I could, but still near enough to her that she blew smoke in my face.

"I have something I need you to sign." I handed the form to her.

She grabbed it out of my hand like a spiteful child. "What is this?"

"It lets you know where I'll be when I leave." I stated in a business-like manner.

She looked over it, I don't know how much she read before she responded. "So now you're moving in with him! You know God won't be happy. You're just paving your own path to hell. You know that?"

"You can sign it or not. Either way, I'll be leaving eventually." I handed her a pen.

She begrudgingly signed the form and tossed it back to me. "You know you're slowly killing me." I was used to her drama, but that was a new one.

"When do you plan on moving in with him?" She spat.

"I haven't decided yet. I have time. I just wanted to let you know it'll be happening." I had just taken the first step in controlling my own life; it was extremely satisfying and exhilarating.

Chapter Twenty-Four

I came home a few days later and found an envelope attached to the front door. I wondered where my mom and grandma were, since if they were home, they would have gotten the notice. I removed it, took it inside with me, sat at the dining table and read it. I realized I was home alone as I looked over the note. The first thing I saw was that it was from the property management company that owned our rental. When I saw that, it dawned on me that the "for sale" sign that had been in the front yard for the past few months was no longer there.

My heart sank as I began to read. It was an eviction notice. The duplex we were renting had been sold. We had thirty days to find another place to live. My mom was in no condition to find us a new place to live, she couldn't even get us groceries. I gathered the notice and my keys before walking back out the door. I went directly to the property management company.

I was only seventeen and shouldn't have had to be dealing with finding a new house for my family, but that's exactly what I was doing. It cemented in my mind all the more that I needed to move out and spend my last year in high school as a kid, not an adult.

I tried my best to look mature when I walked in to the office by standing up straight, keeping my shoulders back and speaking with a clear, strong voice. "Hi. I just came home to find this eviction notice on my family's door. What can we do to get another place to live?"

The woman at the desk was skeptical. "Shouldn't your parent be here doing this?"

"Yes she should, unfortunately she is not feeling well." I replied, trying to sound like an adult.

"Okay, let me see. What do you need?" she asked me.

"We'll need at least three bedrooms and two bathrooms for the same rent that we are currently paying." I was proud of how adult I sounded.

"That's fine. We will just need a deposit as well as first and last month's rent."

My mom didn't have that kind of money in the bank, she probably had no money in the bank. We pretty much survived paycheck to paycheck. "Since we already rent property with you, we already paid a first and last month's rent and we already paid for this month and we have to be out by the end of the month. Can you just use that for the last month on a new property and use the security deposit you already have from us? "

"I don't see why not, unless we need to use some of the security deposit to clean up after you move out of the current property. Then we would need you to make up that difference."

"We can do that." I agreed.

"Let me see what we have available in the next few weeks." She began to look through files while I waited patiently. "We have a three bedroom, two bath house coming available in the next couple weeks. Would you like to drive by and let me know if you want it?"

"We'll take it. What's the address though, I'd still like to drive by."

She wrote the address on a piece of paper and handed it across the desk to me. "Here you go."

"Will we be able to move in before we have to be out of our current place?" I wanted to make sure we'd be able to be out of our house in time.

"Yes. It should be ready for move in three weeks from yesterday. Let me give you some paperwork that your mom will have to fill out and get back to us as soon as possible so that we don't rent it to somebody else."

"Thank you so much. I'll try to get this back to you later today. You close at five, right?"

"Yes."

"Thank you!" I said again as I left the office. That was a success, I thought to myself. I felt again like I was the adult in the family, making sure that we had a place to live. I was proud of myself for negotiating a place to live, but I was also angry that I had to deal with it.

By the time I walked back in the door at home, my mom was back in her usual spot across from the door, on the couch, smoking her beloved cigarette and my Grandma was in her chair across from the couch. I handed my mom the letter as I walked past her to my bedroom. I gave her a few minutes to read it, then went back to her and my Grandma to let them know what I did to take care of us.

"I already got us another rental. They'll use the last month's rent from this place and we can give them first month's rent at the beginning of the month. They'll also use the security deposit that we get back from here towards the new place. If they need to use any of it to clean here, we'll have to make up the difference." I did my best explaining to her what I has worked out.

My Grandma responded first, "that sounds like a good plan, Mishell." laughing nervously as she finished.

"Thank you, Grandma." I knew my Grandma loved me.

"You made a plan without talking to me about it? What if the house isn't big enough for us? What if it's a horrible mess? And we better get the deposit back for this place because I have no money to make up any difference! I can't believe you'd do that!"

Anger bubbled in me threatening to flow out in hurtful words to her. It took tremendous effort to not blow up at her. "I did what I thought needed to be done. Should I have waited for you to go to the office and take care of it? We'd never have another place if I had done that."

"Whatever!" she turned away from me petulantly, like a child, upset by her restrictions.

I returned to my bedroom and called my dad, I told him that we had to move and asked him to help. He agreed and we set a date for it.

At the end of July, about the same time as the eviction notice, I started my senior year. I had decided that when we moved I would begin taking my things to Paul's house. I was counting down the days until I would no longer be living with my mom.

The class I was most interested in was the nurse's assistant class. The class was the first two periods of the day and took place at another school site. There was a lot to learn, but I knew that it was leading me in the right direction to accomplish my ultimate goal of becoming a nurse. I had to learn medical terminology, basic anatomy and physiology, patient care and the list went on and on. I totally understood why it was two periods every day. Besides the classroom stuff, we were doing hands on training at a local convalescent hospital a couple of days a week. I even had to buy a nurse's uniform. I was proud of taking charge of my future.

The rest of my classes, weren't so exciting or useful, so there were many days that I would not go back to school after the CNA class. I'd go spend the day with Paul instead. I managed to get most of my absences excused by writing notes that I signed my mom's name on. She had been having me sign everything for school since the year before, for my siblings and myself, because she was too shaky when she tried to write.

My counselor called me in to her office one day to talk to me. "Please take a seat, Mishell," pointing to a chair near her desk as she closed the door. 'So, how are you? I know you were having a hard time near the end of the year last year."

I appreciated that she remembered that about me. I knew she had hundreds of students to keep track of and it made me feel special that I was worth her time and attention. She was one more person who saw me as important, that list was growing all the time. "Things are a lot better. I broke up with Jay, which was hard."

"You had been dating him for a while, what made you break up with him?" She seemed genuinely interested.

I shifted uncomfortably in the hard chair. I knew I could trust her, but I didn't know if I wanted to say it again. I decided I would. "I broke up with him because he raped me." I kept my eyes on my lap the entire time, tears filling my eyes.

"I'm so sorry, Mishell." She awkwardly put a hand on my shoulder. Her compassion made me cry more. She handed me a tissue. "Have you told anybody else?"

I wiped the tears from my eyes. "My new boyfriend and his family knows and my mom."

"Did any of them file a police report?"

"No." I replied, shaking my head from side to side.

"Alright." She paused and wrote something down. "How are your classes going this year? I know you struggled with Algebra II last year. How is it this year?"

She was changing the subject, but I could sense she still cared. "I'm getting help in math this year and it's going better."

"That's good. I need to take care of some things about what you just told me about your ex-boyfriend. Are you okay with that? Do you need to talk some more?"

"No, I think I'm okay." I wiped the last tears away.

"I'm going to send you back to class now. Are you ready?"

Her concern for me was amazing. "I'm fine. I'll be okay."

She handed me a pass back to class. "Come see me any time you need to talk."

"Thank you." I truly appreciated her concern for me. It helped me feel more and more as though I wasn't worthless; that there was a possibility that I could be loved. I smiled as I walked back to class.

The next day I went straight home after school because we were preparing to move so I needed to help pack up our belongings. When I walked through the door my mom was poised to attack before I even had the door closed behind me. "Why weren't you at school this morning?" she screeched.

"What are you talking about? I was at school this morning!" I yelled right back at her.

"Let's just calm down." Grandma interjected.

"Well," my mom continued in a quieter tone, "a police officer went to Dustin's house looking for you because you weren't at school when they looked for you there. Why are police looking for you?"

Shocked, "I have absolutely no idea why cops would be looking for me." I couldn't figure out why they'd be looking for me. I hadn't done anything wrong, except skip classes, but I really was there that morning. "I was in class today and nobody at school told me that police wanted to talk to me. I never got called to the office." I was completely baffled.

"You better figure it out tomorrow. While you're at it, you can give the school our new address. We'll be moving this weekend."

"I'll do my best to figure it out." I told her before heading down the hall to my room.

I grabbed a few boxes and starting packing my stuff. I labeled each box with my name. In the new house, I planned on just keeping things packed so it would be easier to take them to Paul's a little bit at a time. When I finished packing all my belongings except clothes, I turned to homework. I struggled with the math first before tackling the rest. I finished and was just lying on my bed waiting until I could go see Paul.

Suddenly my bedroom door opened and my mom stood in the doorway, one hand on the doorknob and the other on her hip. "Who called the police? Did Paul's mom do it? What did you say to her?" Her speech was slow and deliberate.

"I don't know who called the police. I don't know why anybody would call the police." I answered honestly, annoyed by her interruption of my time.

"I'll bet it was her. I bet you told her what a horrible mother I am and she turned me in." Her hand left her hip and she was wagging a pointing finger at me. "This is all your fault!"

"I didn't tell her anything." I protested.

Finger still wagging in my direction. "You told her enough that she wants you to come live with them. You made me sign that paper. You obviously told her something!"

"Nothing that would make her call the police. Besides you signed the paper. I can move in with them whenever I'm ready." I may be ready sooner than later with this behavior.

"She hates me, I know. She wants to destroy me." She seemed completely paranoid to me, thinking Paul's mom was out to get her.

"She doesn't want to destroy you, Ma. Please stop. She just wants to help me. I'll figure this out tomorrow when I get to school." I tried to calm her down.

"You need to call her, right now and ask her if she called the police on me." Her words were coming faster, like water flowing downstream.

"No! I won't accuse her of that!" I argued.

"You love her more than you love me, is that it? You're trying to protect her. Call her to prove me wrong." She was antagonizing me, trying to start trouble between Paul's family and me.

"No. I won't do it!" I put my pillow over my face to drown her out.

"It's fine. I know the truth. You love her more than me." With that she left me alone.

I knew Paul's mom didn't call the police. If she was going to do that she would have done it a long time ago and she would tell me. My mom was making it tremendously difficult to want to stay with her. I also knew my mom wouldn't believe that it wasn't Paul's mom unless I did call her. I mean I could just tell her that I asked, but I didn't want to lie to my mom. As angry as she made me, I didn't want to be in the wrong so, I made the call.

I dialed their number and waited for the call to be answered. I was extremely nervous. I didn't want to accuse her of anything. "Hello." She Answered.

"Hello. It's Mishell." I started, not knowing how to start.

"Oh, hi. Paul's not home right now." She replied.

"I know. I called to talk to you." I still didn't know what I was going to say.

"Okay. What's going on?" She sounded confused.

"Well my mom wants me to ask you something. She wants to know if you called the police on her for anything I've told you." I blurted before I chickened out.

"The police? No, I didn't call the police. Why would she think that?" I could hear the shock in her voice

"I don't know. An officer came to talk to me today, but I wasn't there and don't know what he wanted so she's being paranoid. I'm sorry I called." I apologized.

"It's okay, Mishell." She reassured me.

"Thank you. Bye." I said.

"Bye."

When I hung up I walked to the living room and found my mom, on the couch as usual. "I just got off the phone with Paul's mom. She didn't call the police."

"She's probably lying to you. She just doesn't want you to know. She just wants to take you away from me." Nothing was going to make her believe me.

"I can't convince you otherwise. I'm leaving. I'll be home by ten." I went straight to Paul's house.

The next day at school, I went to the office before I left campus for my CNA class. I informed them of our new address and asked about the police officers looking for me the day before. The officers had come to talk to me while I was off campus in my CNA class, that's why I wasn't at school, but the secretaries had no idea why the police wanted to talk to me.

When I walked into the house after school that day, my mom informed me that since I had cut school the day before, I would be spending the next two days with my dad cleaning our new house. I tried to explain what had happened, that they came while I was off campus, but she didn't believe me. That frustrated me; I may have not been the daughter she expected or wanted recently, but I was not a liar!

The next morning, I drove my brother to my dad's house as usual to catch the bus to his junior high. Then I took Stefyni to school before meeting my dad at our new house.

He was there with all the cleaning supplies we could possibly need to make the house livable. That was good because it was pretty disgusting. I don't know how the property management company could charge us a cleaning fee. The walls were filthy, the cabinets weren't even empty, there was food crumbs and scraps in the sink and on the counters. It would take me all of the two days to clean the filth, if not more.

My dad stayed long enough to tell me how to clean the house, as if I couldn't see what needed to be bleached. Everything!

He left me alone to work. When I was ready for a break I sat outside to escape the noxious fumes of the cleaning supplies. While I was out breathing in the fresh air, a police car parked in front of the house. An officer got out of the car and began to walk towards me. Perfect, I thought, I'll finally figure out what this is all about.

"Hello." The officer began. "Are you Mishell?"

"Yes, I am." Suddenly nervous.

"Are your parents here?"

"No. My dad left me to work here." I explained. I probably told him more than he cared to know, but I was nervous.

"Can we go inside and talk?" He motioned to the door.

"Sure, but it smells like bleach." I led him inside, leaving the door open to let some of the bleach smell out.

"Is there somewhere less toxic?" he laughed.

"Let's see." I took him to what would be my Grandma's bedroom because I hadn't started in there yet. We stood near the open window to get fresh air.

The officer removed a notepad from his front shirt pocket, along with a pen. "You're a difficult person to find, Mishell. I've been to your school and a house around the corner from here trying to find you. Glad I finally tracked you down."

I smiled nervously, "the first time I was in a class off campus and then we're moving." I didn't know how much to say.

"Why are you here instead of at school today?" He questioned, poised to write down pertinent information.

"My mom thinks I skipped school because you couldn't find me there the other day. My punishment is to spend today and tomorrow cleaning this house so we can move in this weekend." I was probably saying too much. I had never been questioned by police before.

"I see. Do you know why I want to talk to you?"

"No. I don't." I shook my head side to side as I answered.

"Well, seems you told your school counselor that an ex-boyfriend of yours raped you."

My eyes grew big as saucers. I did this. I started this. This was all my fault because I told. "Yes. I talked to her about that."

"We need to make a police report." He informed me.

"Alright." I sounded more sure than I felt. My insides were quivering with every heartbeat.

"Let's start with his name."

"Jay."

"His full name, please." I told him and he wrote it down as I spelled it for him.

"Do you know where he is now?"

"No, I don't. He's in the Marines. Last I knew he was in San Diego." I answered.

"I'm not going to ask you for any details, but I do need to ask a few more questions." I nodded while he continued. "How old were you when this happened?"

"I was fifteen." He made a note.

"How old was he and when did this happen?" He asked.

"He was eighteen. It happened May 6, 1990. Well that was the first time." I shuddered at the memory of that afternoon.

"Did he force you to have sex with him?"

"Yes."

"You said the first time. Did it happen more than once?" I nodded. "When did you break up with him?"

"This past April." I admitted, hanging my head and refusing to look at the officer.

"That's eleven months after he allegedly raped you. Why'd you take so long to say anything? Why'd you stay with him?"

I was embarrassed. It was my fault. If I had just broken up with him sooner, he wouldn't have continued mistreating me. "Once he did it, I didn't care anymore." I whispered the answer, totally defeated.

"Well, since you stayed with him for so long afterwards we can't say that he raped you. Maybe statutory rape since he was eighteen and you were fifteen. And given the fact that he's in the Marines, I doubt this'll go anywhere. Thank you for your time." He handed me a business card before leaving. I stood rooted to the spot, shocked by what he said.

Because I stayed with him, because I didn't break up with him right away, because I was embarrassed and ashamed of what Jay did to me, he wouldn't have to answer for it. The officer made it sound like it was all my fault. That I must have wanted it since I stayed with him for eleven more months before breaking up with him. I hated myself. I felt dirty and betrayed again. The words flooded my mind.

Slut.
Whore.
Idiot.
Garbage.
Heathen.
Sinner
Lonely.
Stupid.
Worthless.

Each word hit me like a hammer striking a nail, driving home a point. Everything that happened to me was my fault. If I had not let Jay touch my breasts that first night. If I had not let him put his finger inside me. If I had not let him force me into having sex. Too many ifs. I hated myself!

The words kept running through my mind as the tears fell; I collapsed into a heap on the floor. I was crying for everything bad that had ever happened to me. I was crying for everything I thought my parents should have been for me. I was crying for the things I wanted to accomplish, but felt unable to do. I was crying for who I could be without these words constantly coming back to haunt me, always there in the back of my mind, ready to sabotage me every time I began to take charge of my own life.

After feeling sorry for myself for some time, I got back to work. I had to stay at the house and clean until my dad came back to allow me to go home. As I continued to scrub and clean the house, I began to see things in a new light. When I arrived that morning, the house was disgusting. I didn't even want to be in it. However, after all the work I'd been doing, it was looking like it could be lived in. It was cleaning up very nicely. I was proud of what I had accomplished there.

The words I used that morning to describe the house were negative; filthy, disgusting, horrible, stinky, appalling, repulsive. Now the words I would use to describe it were much more positive; clean, comfortable, bright, roomy.

The house wasn't perfect yet, there was still a lot of work to do before we could move in to it that weekend, but it was improving. That was the same with me. I wasn't perfect, but I was improving, my life was getting better. My life didn't fall apart overnight and I couldn't expect it to get better overnight. It was going to be a process and I needed to remember that, when the negative words and thoughts tried to sneak back in to pull me down I just needed to remind myself of the positive words that could define me and that I was a work in progress. I had people in my life who loved and accepted me and I needed to focus on them, instead of worrying about earning love from my parents.

Of course, this was easier said than done. When my dad came back to release me to go home, he began to look around. He inspected what I had done in the kitchen and instead of telling me what I did well, he picked it apart. I apparently hadn't done anything right. According to him, I was useless. The house was still a disaster area and I was completely incompetent. He yelled for a few minutes, ranting and raving as he inspected everything I did and didn't get to that day.

I repeated my new mantra in my head, "I'm a work in progress. I'm a work in progress. I'm a work in progress."

He finally stopped cutting me down and let me leave for the day. I had to go straight home because I was grounded for cutting school. It was cruel and unusual punishment; I was being forced to sit in a house with a woman (my mom) who smoked nonstop. Our walls were yellow with nicotine and I didn't want my lungs to look that way too. I was also being forced to clean these walls once we moved out on Saturday. I was being punished for skipping school on a day when I was actually there; it was laughable.

I managed to hideout in my room for the entire evening and avoid my mom and her cigarette smoke. The next day, I once again, spent the day cleaning the new house so we could move in on Saturday. Once again, while I was impressed with the transformation of the house from a dump into a home, my dad found every flaw. I didn't let it bother me, I would be moved out by the end of August.

Since I was grounded when we moved, I had to move all my things with me to the new house instead of to Paul's. While Stefyni unpacked her things, I left all of mine in boxes in the closet. I wasn't staying at this house long enough to unpack. I didn't get any rest that weekend, I moved and cleaned the old house, collapsing into bed exhausted each night. I was so thankful to go back to school on Monday morning.

My dad had left a note with my mom for me to give the school explaining my two-day absence. It read: "Please excuse Mishell's absences. She was cleaning a rental house." Finished it with his signature. I took it straight to the office when I got to school. Unfortunately for me, cleaning a rental was not an excused absence so I would have to go to Saturday school so that my grades would not be affected by unexcused absences.

I left the office shaking my head. I was assigned Saturday school because my dad made me stay home and clean a house. I never had to go to Saturday school for all the days I skipped school to hang out with Paul. The only time I got in trouble by my parents for cutting school was when I was actually there. It was so ridiculous, it made me laugh.

Chapter Twenty-Five

I may have been grounded, but that did nothing to keep me from seeing Paul. He often worked late, so I'd sneak out and spend time with him in the middle of the night. I'd go to bed about nine o'clock, making my mom happy that I was finally being a "good girl." Then a little before midnight I'd climb out of bed, grab my clothes for school the next day and make sure Stefyni was asleep.

I'd hear Paul's car and I would slip out into the hallway which is where my closet was. I'd open it as quietly as I could and grab something to leave at Paul's house. Next, I'd take three steps down the hall to the door leading to the garage, sneak through it without making a sound and set my school clothes on the dryer before walking out the side door of the garage. I'd walk down to the sidewalk to where Paul would be waiting for me.

Some nights we'd find somewhere to park and talk and other nights we'd drive around. One night we parked in an empty parking lot, turned the music up and danced beside the car. I thoroughly enjoyed every minute I could spend with Paul, even if I was having to sneak out to do it.

About four-thirty in the morning Paul would drive me back to my house. I'd slip back in the side door to the garage, grab my clothes from the dryer and walk into the house. If my mom was awake and caught me, she would just think I was up early getting my laundry and I'd head straight to the shower. If she was still asleep, I could get about an hour's sleep before I had to get up for school. I was able to sneak out just about every night while I was grounded.

When I finally got done being grounded, I decided to stay the night at Paul's house to get a feel for what it would be like to live there. I spent the day with Paul, had dinner with the family and was still there when it was time for bed. It seemed weird, but comfortable doing this totally normal, everyday thing with his family. I was sharing a bathroom with Paul and his brother so we had to work that out. After I had brushed my teeth I said goodnight to his parents. I met Paul in the hallway between our bedrooms. We kissed good night and went to our separate rooms. I fell asleep thinking about how much this family meant to me.

I felt at home here, it was a feeling I had spent so much of my life trying to earn from my family. Paul's family accepted me for who I was, not like my parents who only accepted me when I was doing what they wanted me to do. Even then they made sure that I understood that I wasn't good enough. Both my mom and dad had told me, at different times and more than once, that the only reason they had children was to take care of them. I know many parents say that jokingly with their kids, but the way my parents behaved towards us and the demands they placed on is, I totally believed them.

I slept well that night and woke up in the morning completely refreshed. I looked in the closet and saw some of my things were already in there. Only my clothes and one box of my personal items were left at my house. I smiled as I ran my fingers over my prom dress hanging in the closet, remembering the amazing night we had for my Junior prom. I really did love Paul and his family.

Unfortunately, I couldn't stay wrapped up in the coziness of Paul's family just yet, I had to go back home that morning. I still had a few things that had to be moved over.

When I arrived home later that morning, I escaped to the sanctuary of my bedroom as soon as I walked in the door. I didn't have much to do, so I did what I do best, think. I thought about Jay and how I had compromised so much of myself to have a boyfriend, a Christian boyfriend to make my mom happy. I allowed him to touch me, even though I was uncomfortable with it, which eventually led to him raping me, which made me feel even worse about myself and I gave up.

I gave up everything; my body, my joy, my worth, my dignity. Most of it was gone before I even met him, but he destroyed any hope I had of being valuable and loved. I had thought that having a boyfriend would help me feel better about myself, but it didn't work that way. I ended up not wanting this life anymore.

Then I found the words to describe what Jay had done to me and I got some of my power back. I began to realize that I defined my worth, not others. Over the past eight months or so I had taken charge of my life and how I would live it. In most ways it was liberating. I felt free. I knew that no matter what, God loved me. I didn't have to follow all the rules my mom and the church made in order for God to love me. He already did.

The most difficult part of all of it was that I still, so badly, wanted my mom to love and accept me. I felt better about myself with the way things were going, but I still didn't understand why she couldn't just love me? She was my mom. That was kind of in the job description, wasn't it? Weren't parents supposed to love their kids no matter what? Since I broke up with Jay all my mom and I did was fight, bring Paul into the picture and she acted as if I was dancing with the devil, literally.

I had finally found a place that felt like home and a family that loved and accepted me as their own, but it wasn't enough. I still needed my mom to love me. I still needed her approval. I still wanted to be mommy's girl and be special to her. I had hope. If a family that wasn't even my own flesh and blood could love me, maybe my mom could too. The problem was, I would have to make a difficult choice; my mom would never love me if I was dating Paul.

To gain her love I would have to give up the person I loved. The person who helped me find my voice and regain my power. The person who helped me learn to love myself. The person who knew everything about me and loved me anyway. I knew that I would have to give all that up to get my mom's love. That would be a difficult decision.

If I chose Paul, I would lose my parents. All I ever wanted was for my parents to love me. When I was dating Jay, my mom acted like she cared about and loved me. I was miserable though. I stayed with him just so my mom would love me. Now I was happy with myself. I was happy with Paul. I was doing alright in school, but my mom hated me.

If I chose my mom, I would have to lose Paul. There was no way that she would ever accept him or me with him. I would lose the most important person in my life. I would be losing a person that I knew loved me in the hope of having my mom love me. I would be losing a sure thing for a gamble. My mom may never love me.

What would happen though if Paul's family changed their minds about me and didn't want me to live with them anymore? I would have nowhere to go. My mom would certainly never let me move back home. She made that clear since I had her sign the paper. Then there was always a possibility of Paul breaking up with me. I mean we're in love, but young. What are the chances that we'd actually make it? If we broke up, I'd have nobody.

I hated this. I hated that I needed her love. I hated that I would have to make this decision. I hated that I felt so much love with Paul and his family and I didn't feel it at home. I hated that my mom hated me. I hated that her love was conditional. I hated that she used religion to treat me and others badly. I hated how judgmental she was. I hated to admit that I knew what my decision would be.

I cried. For all that I was losing, I cried. For all that I was hoping for, I cried. For a chance at a new life, I cried. For all that was in my past, I cried. For all the years I lost trying to be loved, I cried. I cried and cried and cried until I was spent and had no more tears to shed, no more energy to give. I cried.

When I was done, I laid in my bed, exhausted, puffy red eyes, stuffy nose and tear stained cheeks. Crying hadn't made the decision any easier to deal with. It hadn't made me love Paul any less. It hadn't made my mom love me. Crying hadn't accomplished anything. I was still blessed with the thought of a family who loved me and plagued with thoughts of my own family who didn't. I was still alone. I still hurt. I still had to make a decision.

It was the most difficult decision I ever had to make. I had no idea if I was making the right choice. I felt either choice left me at a loss; either I'd lose Paul and his family or I'd lose my family. At the moment, I knew my mom and dad didn't love me, but because Paul's family did, I had hope that my parents could love me too.

Breaking up with Paul was horrible. It was difficult. It was emotional. It felt like I was ripping my own heart out of my chest. I'm pretty sure that Paul felt the same way. So many times, I wanted to tell him I changed my mind, but whenever I started to waver in my decision my mom was there cheering me on; telling me that I was doing the right thing, that she was proud of me for making the decision.

She was rooting for me to destroy the heart of the guy I loved. I knew she was wrong about him, but I wanted her affection so badly that I refused to work it out with Paul. I even started dating a guy from youth group to show my mom how committed I was to doing things the "right" way. She just cheered louder. She began inviting him over when I wasn't home to get to know him better. She was taking an interest in me again.

While on the outside I seemed to have everything together, dating a Christian, attending youth group and church, and generally obeying all my mom's and God's rules, I was not entirely happy. There was a part of me that hated what I did to Paul. A part of me still loved him and probably always would. I knew I had made the wrong choice, but it was too late to change it now. I believed that I'd never be able to love anybody as much as I loved Paul.

Since I couldn't change my mind now, I had already hurt Paul, I poured all my energy into being the "perfect" daughter and girlfriend to Parrish. I began to hang out at home more to keep my mom happy. I helped her even more with cooking and running errands. I quit fighting with her so much. Instead of telling her how I thought or felt about things if they contradicted her, I kept my opinions to myself. I wanted her to love me after all, and that love was still conditional. I still had to earn it.

Chapter Twenty-Six

Parrish and I got to know each other. We hung out after school most days. He wanted to be a paramedic-firefighter and I wanted to be a nurse. He enjoyed hunting and fishing, two things I had never done before. He was two years older than me and attending a nearby junior college. He was a volunteer firefighter for a local, rural fire department. The thing that was best, in my mom's opinion, was that he was a Christian and attended the same church I did.

In the beginning of the relationship things were going well. We enjoyed spending time together, either at my house or his. It was nice, but I constantly compared how I felt to my relationship with Paul. He knew that my break up with Paul was hard, he even witnessed some of it. I could never talk to him about any of those feelings. If I brought Paul up in conversation, he would get agitated, even if I just told him about somewhere Paul and I had gone. I quickly learned that Paul was a secret that I had to keep in a section of my heart that was off limits if others were around.

Parrish was always at my house when I got home from school, visiting with my mom and grandma. They loved it, which helped my mom love me. He'd greet me with a hug and kiss on the cheek, then we'd go to another room to talk and do homework together. He'd talk about his fire science classes and do his best to help me with math and chemistry.

On one afternoon, I told him about the group of people that I ate lunch with. (Since I had broken up with Paul I had to find a new group of friends because all my old friends sided with him. Another blaring reminder that I had made the wrong choice.) Included in that group of new friends were three girls and two guys. Parrish began to quiz me about the guys in the group and I honestly didn't know a whole lot about them, just that they were friends of my friends. The girls in the group had been acquaintances of mine since junior high. I liked and trusted them so I trusted the guys too.

Parrish grew irritated. "Just to inform you, high school guys that hang out with girls are either gay or they want to hook up with the girls. Neither of which is okay with me."

"Well, getting to know them the past few weeks, I don't think they're gay or want to hook up with us." I argued.

"It wasn't all that long ago that I was a high school guy. Trust me, I know what I'm talking about. I don't trust them and I don't like you hanging out with them." He stared at me.

"It's just at lunch. I don't have anybody else to eat with." I was being whiny about it. I didn't want to eat alone and let all my old friends know that I had nobody at school since I broke up with Paul.

"I'd just rather you didn't eat with the guys." He continued.

I changed the subject then and put the focus back on homework. I needed to finish it. If I failed Chemistry I wouldn't be able to graduate at the end of the year. I figured the issue was done. I wasn't going to eat lunch alone.

About a week later, when I walked through the door, Parrish was there on the couch, waiting for me as usual. We went to the table to start homework and he started in again on the same thing. "Are you still having lunch with those two guys?"

"I still eat with the whole group." I answered. Not thinking anything of it.

"You still sit with them even though you know I don't like it?"

"Yeah. They don't like me and they're not gay. I don't see the problem." I had already given up a guy friend that I had known since junior high for Jay and I didn't want to give up friends for Parrish.

"You're my girlfriend. When you said yes to that it meant that you'd agree to not do things that made me uncomfortable." He tried to explain to me.

I didn't know that was part of the agreement. "Really?"

"Yes. It's part of being committed to someone. You're not going to do things that they are uncomfortable with."

I shook my head; I couldn't believe I was agreeing to this, again, but I wanted to stay in my mom's good graces. "Alright. I'll stop eating lunch with them." I knew if I broke up with him after such a short time, my mom would not forgive me. It seemed that she already liked him.

So, the next day at lunch I made an excuse to my friend's and went to the library. I did that again the day after that and the day after that until they didn't expect me to sit with them at lunch anymore. I sat by myself in a cubicle desk, eating my lunch without any friends, to keep a new boyfriend happy.

After a few days, I decided to read the Bible during lunch. I could learn more about God and that should make Him happy. One day as I was reading I came across the "Love" chapter, First Corinthians chapter thirteen verses four to eight:

"4 Love is patient, love is kind. It does not envy, it does not boast, it is not proud. 5 It does not dishonor others, it is not self-seeking, it is not easily angered, it keeps no record of wrongs. 6 Love does not delight in evil but rejoices with the truth. 7 It always protects, always trusts, always hopes, always perseveres. 8 Love never fails." (New International Version)

When I finished the verses, I stopped and thought about Parrish. Did I love him? Was romantic love defined in these verses? Could I love someone again after Paul? If I defined romantic love by these verses, I could be in love with

Parrish. I continued to think about it throughout the rest of my school day.

Once again, when I arrived home that afternoon, Parrish was waiting for me. As soon as I closed the door behind me he reached for my hand and began to pull me down the hall to my room. "I have to talk to you!"

I was a little worried. He seemed intense. "Okay." I replied as we entered my bedroom. We left the door open per my mom's rules and he sat down at the foot of my bed. I sat up near my pillows and pulled one onto my lap. "What's up?" I started.

"Well, today at lunch I was reading my Bible." His eyes searched mine.

"Really? Me too." I started to say more, but he cut me off.

"Anyway," He waved his hand as if to shoo away what I had been about to say. "I was reading in first Corinthians, the chapter about love."

Wary, "Me too."

"Okay, so after reading that I think I love you. I love you, Mishell. I love you like the Bible talks about." The words spilled out.

Fireworks exploded in my heart. He just told me that he loved me. "That's the same exact chapter I was reading today at lunch and I was thinking about you while I read it." I wanted him to know.

"God put us together. He made us read the same chapter at the same time. That's not just a coincidence. We are meant to be together."

I couldn't argue that it seemed like more than a mere coincidence that we had read the same bible passage at almost the same time and thought about each other while reading it. "You're right. God is in this relationship. I love you too." I didn't love him the same way that I had loved

Paul, but I did love him according to the Bible passage we read that day.

Parrish scooted closer to me on the bed and reached across the empty space between us to wrap me in a hug. It was sweet. Then he kissed me on the cheek. "I love you, Mishell!"

"I love you too, Parrish!" In my head, I finished the statement with, "but not as much as I love Paul."

I started seeing Parrish in September, just a little over a month after we moved in to our new house. By Christmas, we were moving again with the help of Parrish and Dustin. This house was owned by my Grandma on my dad's side. She wasn't going to charge us rent, which was a great gift to my family. My mom was now on permanent disability and the payments weren't very much. My Grandma who lived with us had been helping with the rent, but she was moving to Phoenix with one of my aunts so we wouldn't have help for rent, the bills or food.

This was the nicest house we had ever lived in. It had four bedrooms which meant that Stefyni and I would have our own rooms for the first time in our lives. It was a somewhat sad experience as we divided our belongings and it was hard to fall asleep the first few nights without her there to talk to. It was nice however, to be able to be alone in my room during the day especially when Parrish came over and we wouldn't be interrupted by my sister, even though we still had to leave the door open so nothing "bad" could happen.

I didn't worry about that with him. He didn't pressure me at all to have sex with him, or to do anything more than kiss. I was the one whose hands tended to roam during make out sessions, while he was the one asking me to slow down and I respected that. The last Christian I had dated was Jay and he always pressured me to go further sexually than I wanted to. Paul had never pressured me, and Parrish wasn't either.

At school, I began to eat lunch with my group again, I just didn't tell Parrish about it. I was also making more friends at church. Well, both of us were. We were friends with people that Parrish wanted to be friends with. I didn't really care who I was friends with, at least I was making more friends.

A few months after we moved into the new house we got a new youth pastor at church. He was also the owner of a company that cleaned rental properties before the next tenants moved in and Parrish just happened to work for him.

When he took over the youth group, he started a leadership group, to train leaders and have helpers in the youth group. Parrish and I were both chosen to be part of the group as well as ten other youth that we knew ranging in age from junior high to college age. I was one of only three girls chosen to be a part of the group. I was a valuable asset to the group because I was chosen for a leadership role.

This group became our closest friends. One of the other girls became my best friend and two of the guys became Parrish's best friends. We hung out a lot with the two guys outside of youth group and church; it seemed they were always with us. I began to feel like one of the guys. It was okay, I rationalized, because at least he wasn't pushing me for sex. He respected me in that area, which was an incredible improvement over the last Christian I dated.

Once we moved into my grandma's house, my mom's health took a turn for the worse. Besides her stomach issues she was now becoming dizzy much of the time. She walked around the house holding onto the walls as she walked just to remain upright. Routinely, she would call each one of us children into her bedroom and tell us her final goodbyes, she was convinced that she was dying. The conversations were usually her telling us how we were messing up and how she thought we could fix it. Then she'd tell us not to be sad when she finally died.

Sometimes my friends were there when she did this and I would be completely embarrassed. She wasn't dying. She was just sick, but the doctors couldn't give us a name for what was making her so ill. It was frustrating to me, so I'm sure it was more so for her. She was depressed and it was affecting all of us; it was pushing me more towards Parrish and forcing me to rely on him more than I wanted too.

That May I graduated from high school. Not one of my family members attended the ceremony. Parrish, his mom and grandma were there. Pastor Tim even drove to Lodi from Santa Rosa to be there. My mom and dad didn't show up. They showed me, once again by their actions, that I was unimportant to them, I didn't matter, and I was worthless.

It was also obvious that I had made the wrong choice. I had given up Paul to gain my mom's love and now I didn't have that either.

About a month after my seventeenth birthday Paul and I had made a plan that on my eighteenth birthday we would go to Disneyland together. It would be my first time there. I secretly hoped that no matter how angry he was with me, or how much I hurt him that he would still show up on the morning of my eighteenth birthday and take me. It didn't happen that way, but I did get to go to Disneyland that summer with the youth group. I had an incredible time, but thought about how it would have been if I was there with Paul instead of the youth group. He was never far from my thoughts, but it was getting less frequent that I let thoughts of him into the forefront of my mind.

After the Disneyland trip, the youth pastor had a swim party at his house. I got permission from my mom to go. I was there having a good time, enjoying myself when his wife came to get me; my mom was on the phone.

"Hello?" as a question. I wasn't sure why she was calling me.

"You didn't do the dishes before you left today." She slurred. She must have been having a dizzy spell.

"I know. I'll do them when I get home tonight." I responded.

"Don't bother coming home tonight or ever again for that matter." She said that as clear as a summer sky. Then she hung up on me.

I set the phone down with a perplexed expression on my face. I couldn't believe she just kicked me out of the house over the dishes not getting done. This was definitely not what I had hoped for when I broke up with Paul. It seemed now that the only way I would escape my mother was with Parrish.

The pastor's wife saw the look of dismay on my face and tried to comfort me. I had nowhere to go. "I can't go home." I said to her as tears filled my eyes.

"What? What's wrong?" She asked, wrapping me up in her arms.

I pulled out of the hug, looked her in the eye, "My mom just told me to never go home again." I was shocked. I had a job interview coming up at the convalescent hospital that I did my CNA training at, but at the moment I didn't have a job. I couldn't afford to pay rent anywhere. I didn't know what I would do.

"You can stay here as long as you need to. We have the guest room you can use."

"Thank you." I said, still not sure of anything.

She called Parrish and the youth pastor into the house and filled them in on what just happened. Parrish decided that he would take me home to get some clothes and hygiene items. I blindly followed him. I couldn't wrap my head around the fact that my mom had just kicked me out of the house. I had given up Paul and she still didn't love me. I was heartbroken.

When I walked into my house with Parrish, my mom was surprised to see me. "I thought I told you not to come home!" she screamed.

"I'm just here to get clothes and my toothbrush and stuff. I'll leave as fast as I can." I walked past her to my bedroom.

"Good and good riddance!" she called after me.

I packed up my clothes and grabbed my toiletries and we left within about fifteen minutes. My mom didn't say another word.

A week later, I was still at the youth pastor's house, when I received a call from my mom. "Where are you? Why haven't you been home all week?"

"You told me to not come home again." I was confused, she didn't remember telling me that?

"I never told you that. Come home, I need you to make me dinner."

"Okay." I agreed, still perplexed.

Parrish drove me home and when I walked in the front door, my mom told me what she wanted for dinner as if nothing had ever happened, as if I had been there all along. It bothered me. I needed to escape from her as soon as possible. I would get a job, save my money, work towards a nursing degree and move out.

Chapter Twenty-Seven

That fall I started attending the local junior college, taking my prerequisite classes for the nursing program and attempting to earn my Associate of Arts degree at the same time. Parrish was still taking classes there as well so we decided to carpool to school together. We managed to get a similar schedule so we could see each other between classes.

Every morning he would come by my house on his way to school and pick me up. Then he decided that to "pay" for the ride I should have breakfast ready for him, he'd just come a little earlier. I thought that it would be no problem, I ate cereal every morning for breakfast, and all I'd have to do is set a bowl out for him too.

The next morning, I was ready for him to come for breakfast. I set out the extra bowl and waited for him to arrive before I ate anything.

I let him in and led him to the kitchen table. I waved my arm like a magician. "Viola, your breakfast is served."

"What, just cereal? I was thinking of eggs and toast." He whined, obviously disappointed in my breakfast preparation skills.

I was deflated. I felt a familiar jab at my worth. The negative thoughts began to flood my mind. I thought I had done something right, and nice and good for Parrish, but I hadn't. He wasn't pleased with my actions and he was letting me know it, by the words he used, the sound of his voice and the look of disappointment that spread across his face.

"I'll make that for you tomorrow. I'm sorry. I just usually have cereal for breakfast and that's what I thought about. I'll make you eggs and toast tomorrow. I promise. I'm so sorry." I was talking so fast it came out as one long run on sentence.

I didn't want to disappoint him. I wanted to do things right for him; to keep him happy with me. My mom already didn't love me and if I lost Parrish, I would be completely alone.

"That sounds nice. Thank you. I like bird in the nest." His voice had changed.

"What is that?" I had never heard of that before.

"You tear a whole in the middle of the bread, then butter both sides. When you've finished doing that you lay it in the hot skillet and crack an egg into the hole in the center. Cook it until the egg is done. The egg is the bird and the bread is the nest." He explained the process well.

"Got it. That will be on the breakfast menu tomorrow morning." That is exactly what I made him for breakfast the next morning and every other morning that he took me to school.

Besides going to college with a fulltime schedule, I had been hired as a Certified Nurse's Assistant, my CNA class had paid off. It was exhausting going to work, doing homework and keeping Parrish happy. I attended school from seven-thirty in the morning until two o'clock in the afternoon. My work hours were from two-forty-five until eleven at night. I worked four days a week and went to school five. I had to do homework on my breaks at work, just to keep up.

Parrish always wanted me to spend non-school and non-work time with him. I never saw my mom anymore. Not that it mattered, she didn't care about me anyway as long as bought the groceries and was home by my curfew.

At college, if I wasn't in class, I was with Parrish. I couldn't make any other friends because he was always there. I realized he monopolized my free time, but figured it was just a part of the relationship; something that I would have to put up with to get the love and attention I desired

It was nice to finally be earning some extra money. I thought I'd be able to save it so that I could eventually move out, but that didn't happen at all. I ended up spending most of it putting gas in my car for work and in Parrish's truck. I also spent a good portion of it on food for Parrish and I and my family. So, even though I had a job, I wasn't any closer to moving away from my mother or her negativity towards me.

As my first year in college continued, my mom added seizures to her list of physical ailments. One afternoon I came home from school to change my clothes before heading to work. Parrish and I walked into the kitchen to find her lying on the floor, unconscious, in a puddle of blood coming from her head. I immediately dialed 9-1-1. Then I called my workplace and told them I had an emergency and I wouldn't be able to come in that day. The charge nurse was disappointed and told me she'd put a note in my file that I didn't give enough notice to call in for time off. I didn't care. I had other things to attend to.

While I was on the phone, Parrish tried to stop the bleeding and see where it was coming from. His emergency medical training was coming in handy. By the time I got off the phone she was regaining consciousness, but seemed to be in a fog.

The paramedics arrived within minutes of my call to them. They assessed her and took her to the hospital to have a thorough examination. I spent the rest of day and well into the night with her in the emergency room. Parrish left when the paramedics left, to do whatever it was that he had planned to do while I was at work that afternoon, so I was on my own with my mom.

We got home from the hospital in the wee hours of the morning. I helped my mom get into bed before collapsing in my own. I had been up for over twenty hours and all I wanted to do was sleep for the few hours I had before I needed to get up for school. However, sleep alluded me. My mind had other plans.

I was mad at myself for caring about my mom when she so obviously didn't care about me. I was a push over, a glutton for punishment. No matter how many times she showed me that she didn't love me, I was still there, doing things, trying to earn her affection. I was even beginning to rethink my career choice. I realized while working at the convalescent hospital that I did not want to be a nurse. That would end up disappointing her as well.

Eventually, I fell asleep. I had just drifted off when I was being shaken awake by my sister. "Something's wrong with Ma! Wake up! She's lying on the floor in the bathroom! Do something!"

I sleepily replied, "It's your turn. I just got home with her a few hours ago. Call 9-1-1." Then I rolled away from her and went back to sleep.

The next thing I knew, there was pounding on the front door, which was just on the other side of the wall from my bed. "Open up! Fire department!"

I pulled the covers over my head and tried to sleep. It didn't happen, but I managed to stay hidden while they evaluated my mom again. And took her to the hospital, again. When they left our house, I called my dad and told him he had to go with her because Stefyni and I had school.

After school that day, I called my sister Cindy to fill her in on the details of our mother's ever worsening health. She had moved the previous year to Portland, Oregon where she had gotten as job as an electron microscopist. That weekend she showed up at our house and took my mom to live with her. She thought it was too much for Stefyni and I to deal with on our own.

So, at eighteen years old, my sister and I were on our own. My brother, who was almost fifteen years old, went to live with our dad while Stefyni and I had the house to ourselves. My dad and my grandma both checked on us regularly and took care of the bills and household maintenance. I ended up quitting my job as a CNA because I hated it and knew that my mom would never love me, even if I became a nurse like she was.

Over the next six to seven months, living on our own, Stefyni and I drifted apart. I was spending all my time with Parrish and the leadership group and she was involved in drama at school and had a job. We rarely saw one another. She graduated from high school and I didn't even go to her graduation. I felt bad, but Parrish wanted to hang out and I figured my future was with him, I needed to keep him happy.

That summer my mom moved back home. She was upset because I had taken over her bedroom when she moved out. My bedroom was at the front of the house, on the street and hers was in the back. I was scared to be home alone in the front so I moved to hers. As soon as she got home she made me move all my belongings back to my room. She was back and in charge. She acted as though she hadn't abandoned us for the last six months. Granted, Cindy had been able to get her to doctors that helped control the symptoms she experienced and she was doing better health wise, but she still had abandoned us.

Within a few weeks, both Stefyni and I found other places to live. She moved into a studio apartment on her own and I moved in with the youth pastor's family since I spent so much time there anyway, and Parrish didn't want me living on my own because I'd have to find a job to be able to afford it. A job would mean that I would have less time to spend with him. I agreed to work as the youth pastor's secretary in exchange for room and board. It seemed like a good deal to me, since Parrish and I already spent a ton of time at the church.

Unfortunately for me, the youth pastor quit in August and would be moving out of town one week before I was supposed to start my second year of college. I was homeless again. I didn't get enough financial aid to pay rent, so I needed to look for a job and a place to live.

I called one of my friends from church because I couldn't get ahold of Parrish when I found this out. I was telling her about my situation and she said she'd talk to her parents to see if they could help. She called me back later and asked me to come to her house and meet her parents, but wouldn't tell me anything else.

I was anxious all afternoon, anticipating going to her house that evening. I had never met her parents before and didn't know what to expect from meeting them.

When I arrived at their house that evening, I needn't have been anxious at all. They welcomed me in with hugs and smiles. They asked me about my college and life goals. I explained to them that I had started college to become a nurse, but that I had decided against that. I didn't know what I wanted to do instead, but that I planned on having my associate's degree by the end of the school year and would continue taking classes until I figured it out. I loved history and other social sciences so I would take as many of those classes as I could.

When that conversation died down, her dad began a new conversation. "Heather told us about your situation and that you need a place to live. It just so happens that we have an extra room upstairs that could be yours if you want it."

"What? I can live here? You don't even really know me." I was completely shocked. I stared at him open mouthed, you could have picked my jaw up off the floor.

"Heather really likes you and you seem like you have a good plan in life. You just need some help." Her mom replied. "So, would you like to live with us?"

"Oh, my gosh, yes!" I wanted to cry. These complete strangers were welcoming me into their home. I still couldn't understand why my mom couldn't make me feel the same way, accepted no matter what. I hugged them both.

We worked out the details, even that Heather's dad would drive me to school when he took her to school, and I moved in a few days later. Immediately, I was a part of the family. I had chores and rules to follow and they allowed Parrish to be there as long as we weren't alone together. He became a part of their family too. I finally belonged somewhere again. It was how I had felt with Paul's family; at home.

Heather's family included me in all their family traditions. At Christmas time, I went along to pick out the Christmas tree. Heather and I got to decorate the tree and the inside of the house. Then two days before Christmas, I was included in their family trip to go shopping in San Francisco. They even gave me an allotment of money to spend on clothes while we were there. I was truly loved and accepted in their family.

On Christmas Eve, Heather and I each slept on a sofa in front of the tree in the living room. When we woke up early the next morning, the tree was surrounded with gifts, even some for me. We raced to the kitchen and quietly fished out pots and metal spoons. Then we tiptoed upstairs to stand outside her parents' bedroom door. We silently counted to three before we started banging the spoons on the pots and shouting that it was Christmas morning and time to get up. They laughed with us as we rushed downstairs to open gifts.

The feelings I experienced that morning will be with me forever. Christmas that morning was by far the best Christmas I had ever experienced up to then. I felt accepted. I felt loved. I felt family. The images from that morning will be forever etched in my memory.

Chapter Twenty-Eight

Winter turned to spring and I was extremely comfortable with my living arrangements. I no longer felt a need to escape anything and my relationship with my mom was getting better, but was still shaky. I was learning to be okay with the fact that she'd never fully love and accept me. I had a family that loved me and I had Parrish, who I would someday start my own family with.

I loved Parrish and I thought our relationship would lead to marriage, but at times it was difficult to stay with him. He would be distant and refuse to talk to me about whatever was bothering him, but no matter what he was always right beside me, never giving me any space.

He monitored my behavior and reprimanded me in front of others if I wasn't behaving according to his expectations. He checked on me at my job to make sure I wasn't flirty with the customers. He was often unhappy with remarks I made about things.

I put up with it because I remembered how he was when we first dated. He was sweet and caring and watched out for me. I figured he was just stressed out about whatever kept him withdrawn from me. If we got married, I believed it would all be okay; I would have a man who loved me and not just a family that accepted me, but my very own family.

On my twentieth birthday, I had to work. It was the first time in my life that I was had to be responsible on my birthday. Having a July birthday meant that I never had to go to school on my birthday and I had never had a job on my birthday before. When I arrived at work that morning my boss had bought a birthday cake for me. I realized that there were a lot of people who cared for me and loved me, even if my mom didn't. I had a good day at work and was able to get off early because Parrish had dinner plans for us.

When I got off work I went home and showered so I wouldn't smell like garlic and raviolis from the deli I worked at. Parrish picked me up right on time and we took off. He hadn't told me where we were going to dinner, it was supposed to be a surprise. Once we were on the freeway he let me know that we were going to an oceanfront restaurant in Monterey.

He had made reservations so when we arrived at the restaurant we were seated immediately. Our table was next to the window overlooking the beach and the Pacific Ocean. The sun setting on the horizon cast orange and pink across the sky that reflected in the water. Dinner was delicious as well. Is was a perfect birthday celebration.

When our dinner plates were taken away, Parrish reached across the table and held both of my hands in his.

"Close your eyes." He told me as he caressed the back of my hands with his thumb.

"Why?" I asked.

"I want to tell you a story and I don't want you to be distracted." He explained.

"Alright." I closed my eyes.

He held my hands as he recounted how we met and the ups and downs we'd experienced over the last three years. I was enjoying the trip down memory lane.

When he was finished reminiscing with me he said, "I want to spend every day with you. Open your eyes."

I slowly opened my eyes and looked directly into his glossy, tear-filled eyes.

"Mishell Renee Allen, I love you and want to spend the rest of my life with you. Will you marry me?"

At that point he looked down at the table and I followed his gaze. There between us was a box containing a diamond solitaire engagement ring.

"Yes." I answered, breathless. "I love you too."

We both stood up and hugged right there in the restaurant. He paid our bill and we left to walk along the beach, which was now bathed in moonlight and the lights from the various buildings that lined the beach. It was a beautiful night. I was getting married.

Eventually we made our way back to his truck and began the drive home. In the dark silence of the vehicle I began to think, always a dangerous undertaking for me.

I looked at him in the lights of oncoming traffic and asked myself if I really wanted to marry him. Did I love him enough to spend the rest of my life with him? Could I trust that once we were married I wouldn't continue to be just one of the guys? Would he finally treat me as though I were special to him?

He did ask me to marry him so that had to mean that I was special to him, right? Besides, if I broke up with him it would hurt too many people. It would obviously hurt the two of us, but it would also hurt his family and our friends. It could hurt his chance at becoming a youth pastor, which is what he wanted to do now. Our friends would have to choose sides and I risked being alone again with no family and no friends if they chose him. Marrying him was the right next step. Everything would work out just fine. I mean we loved each other and that's all we needed. Right?

"What did that sign say?" He broke the silence.

"What sign?" Shaking the negative thoughts from my mind.

"The sign we just passed. Aren't you even paying attention?" His voice gave away his frustration.

"No, I'm not driving." I replied sarcastically.

"You need to let me know where we're going! Let me know that we're headed in the right direction! God, you're useless!"

Tears welled up in my eyes. A single drop made its way down my cheek, landing on the back off my hand in my lap. I looked down and saw the engagement ring, just above where the tear had splashed. I twirled the ring around my finger. It would feel so good to take it off and throw it at him and tell him that I wouldn't marry him. I couldn't marry him. These mood swings were too much to deal with. I didn't want to allow him to belittle me and act like it's all my fault when he was the one who made a mistake instead of taking responsibility for his own actions.

I took the ring off. I had no idea where we were.

"Did you see what that next sign said?" His voice filled the cab of his truck.

"No." I shook my head and looked at the ring in my hand.

"Can't you even tell me where we're going? Don't you know how to get us home from Monterey?" Blaming me for him not knowing where we were going.

"No, I don't know. You drove us here, I figured that you knew how to get us home." I worked hard to keep my voice steady. I didn't want to give away how upset he made me.

"Never mind! I'll figure it out and get us home." He snapped.

I thought about the ring and giving it back him, but if I did that now, while we were driving, I didn't know what he would do. Would he take me home or would he leave me here on the side of the road in his anger? I didn't know what to expect.

I put the engagement ring back on. If I decided to give the ring back to him I'd wait until he dropped me off. Explaining to people that we were engaged would be simple. Most of our friends expected it to happen sooner or later. However, if I gave his ring back to him, that would equate to breaking up with him which would create questions in people's minds and I'd be stuck explaining it over and over. I didn't have the energy for that, besides I wanted to start my own family. I survived my family and they didn't even love me, at least Parrish loved me.

He was going to be a youth pastor. Youth pastors had to be loving and kind, especially towards their wife. He wasn't bad all the time either; only on occasion. Really, the worst he ever did was blame me for his bad moods and mistakes. He had not been as distant in the past few months either, we were connecting better.

I decided that I would marry him. I didn't want to be alone. Once we were married things would be better. He wasn't as bad as Jay, but he wasn't Paul either. That one wrong decision, when I chose my mom over Paul, landed me here. Maybe I didn't deserve to truly be happy.

When I got home, Heather was waiting up so she saw the ring. She reacted exactly how I expected most people would; excited and wondering what took so long. After telling Heather, it became real. I was engaged to Parrish, there was no turning back now.

The whirlwind began the very next day when he decided that the wedding would be in two and a half months. We dated for three years and now he wanted to fast forward to the wedding. I went along with his plan because that's what I did; keep other people happy at the expense of my own happiness. I wanted to put the brakes on and tell him to slow down, but I didn't want to hurt him.

I quickly became caught up in planning a wedding. I asked Stefyni to be my maid of honor and Heather and one other friend to be bridesmaids. Cindy's five-year-old daughter would me my flower-girl. They would all wear teal dresses and carry a candle.

My dress was beautiful. It had a full skirt with lace and sequins around the bottom. It had just a hint of a train with a bow at the back of my waist. The fitted bodice had a sweetheart neckline covered in sequins and lace. The sleeves were a little puffy at the shoulder, tapering down to fit my upper arm where it was decorated with sequins and lace around the edge. The first time I tried it on I felt like a model in a bride's magazine. It was the perfect dress for me.

As the planning went on I was still involved at church. One evening after church I was sitting on a planter bench in the courtyard when a tall, blond woman came and sat beside me.

"Hi! I'm Kim. I hear you need a wedding cake." She didn't even attempt small-talk, just straight to the point. I liked her already.

"Yes, I do. How do you know?"

"My husband is taking classes to get his minister's license with Parrish." She answered

"Oh. Okay. I definitely need a cake. My mother-in-law wants to be involved though. She's going to pay for it." I explained.

"No problem. Why don't the three of you come by my house on Friday and I'll show you pictures of cakes I've done and we can plan yours." She quickly wrote her address on a slip of paper before handing it to me.

"Sounds great! Thank you so much. You have no idea how helpful this is for me. I'm gonna go let Parrish know." With that I left her to tell Parrish the good news.

The planning was done. The wedding would happen. The marriage would be fine.

As we were planning and prepping for the wedding, Parrish and I were getting along much better. It gave me hope for our future together. He was treating me with more respect and taking responsibility for his own actions, instead of blaming me.

The night before the wedding I stayed at my sister Stefyni's apartment along with Cindy, her daughter, Keeth and my mom. I wanted one last night with my family before I began a new family with Parrish. It was a last-ditch effort on my part to make my mom love me.

In the morning, as we were getting prepared to go to the church for the ceremony, my mom caught me alone. "Mishell, I'm proud of your decision. I believe that you marrying Parrish is God's plan for your life. I'm sorry about Jay."

I hugged her. She apologized and she was proud of me. Two of the things I wanted to hear most from her. I believed what she said too, about my marriage being God's will for my life. I chalked up all the reservations I had the night he proposed as cold feet. Parrish was the person I was supposed to be with after all, a Christian man who was going to be a youth pastor.

The ceremony went off without a hitch. At the reception, all our friends and family congratulated us and wished us luck in our new adventure. After a few celebratory hours, we left to enjoy our honeymoon at Disneyland. I couldn't have asked for a more perfect day.

Our honeymoon began with two days at Disneyland, then we just drove north along the California coast on Highway 1. As soon as we left the greater Los Angeles area, the scenery became breathtaking. Most of the highway is built into mountains with cliffs dropping into the Pacific Ocean. The two of us spent hours in the truck talking and enjoying the scenery until we ended up in Pismo Beach, a place I had wanted to visit my entire life.

The two days we spent in Pismo were relaxing, but we had to keep moving because real life awaited us in a few more days. We stayed on Highway 1 and stopped to tour Hearst Castle on our way to Monterey. We spent the last of our honeymoon revisiting where he proposed to me, very romantic. When we left there, Parrish knew how to get us home, and I didn't get blamed once for any bad decisions.

We got along better those seven days than we had been for a while before we got engaged. On our honeymoon, I was no longer one of the guys. It was just him and me, maybe that was all that we had needed, some alone time. We were always surrounded by our youth group friends and we forgot how amazing and comfortable it was when it was just the two of us.

All good things must come to an end, which included our honeymoon. We arrived home to our little apartment to find that Heather's family had moved all my belongings to our apartment while we were gone. I looked at the boxes stacked neatly in the corner and was reminded of how little I owned, it wouldn't take me too long to unpack.

The days and weeks passed. We were adjusting to living together while both maintaining our jobs and attending school. There were days that we only saw each other in passing and would finally snuggle together at the end of a busy day to fall asleep in each other's arms. Other days we could spend time together in the mornings before our days began and again in the afternoons. We prayed together. Somedays Parrish would break out his guitar and we'd have our own little worship service in our living room.

I thought we were adjusting pretty well considering some of the misgivings that I had on the night we were engaged. I even allowed myself to be happy with my new little family. I was sure that we would last forever, there was nothing that would tear us apart. I was finally in a place where I was valued and appreciated.

One evening, when neither of us had class and there was no church we decided to make tacos together for dinner. It was something that we had started cooking together at his house while we were still dating. I cooked the ground beef, shredded the cheese and cut the lettuce, while Parrish fried the tortillas; we had it down to a science.

While the food was cooking, Parrish started conversation with a question. "Do you think we are ever supposed to really be happy?"

I paused before answering, remembering that I used to think that I didn't deserve to be happy, especially after I broke up with Paul. Then I realized how happy I had been since Parrish and I were married a little over two months earlier. "Yes. I think we are supposed to be truly happy."

"I mean now. On this earth. In this lifetime." He sounded like he was lost, struggling to find a way out.

"Yes. I believe we can have true happiness in our lifetime, like right now. I'm happy, married to you, making our favorite meal together."

"I don't know if I can ever be happy." He replied as he placed a fried tortilla on the plate.

"What do you mean?" What was he saying? "You're not happy now? With me?" Shocked.

"No, I'm not really happy. In fact, I regret getting married." He looked into my eyes as he spoke.

"Getting married so young, so quickly or just getting married?" My heart was racing, I had no idea where he was going with this, but I didn't think it was going to end well.

"I regret marrying you." There was no emotion in his voice, his eyes were dull and lifeless.

I was right. It didn't end well. "Are you saying you don't want to be married to me?"

"It's too late now, we're already married." He shrugged his shoulders. "I might as well make the best of it. Maybe I'll eventually be happy with you."

I was relieved that he still wanted to be married and hopeful that he thought he'd eventually be happy. "I'll do my best to make you happy and make sure you don't regret marrying me." I promised him, myself and God that Parrish would see how valuable I could be to him.

Chapter Twenty-Nine

A little over four years had passed since I made that promise. I still knew my worth, but I had failed in making Parrish see my worth as anything more than his helper with the youth group he was now the youth pastor of. At church, we were a perfectly happy couple. We sat together in Sunday services surrounded by the students who attended our junior high youth group. The two of us taught a Sunday school class together. On Wednesday nights, he led worship while I played bass guitar in the band before he preached his sermon. There was also a leadership group that we led on Monday nights that had about twelve students who attended regularly.

Outside of church, our life was a completely different story. Besides being a youth pastor's wife, which was at least a part-time job, I was also a junior high teacher, I was taking five college courses, and I tutored a student at our house twice a week. I was pretty busy and Parrish was busy too.

Besides his job as a youth pastor he was also an administrator at a private elementary school. On Friday evenings, he was often asked, by single moms of our students, to babysit so that they could have an evening out with friends or to go on a date. On Saturdays, he usually went fishing or hunting, sometimes alone, with his mom, or the students.

Outside of church we each had our own, separate life. I wasn't happy with it, but I was getting done what I needed to fulfill my new goal of becoming a high school teacher. I was working towards graduation from Bethany College on May 8, 1999. It was so close. I only had a few more papers to write for a few more classes and I would be finished with the requirements for my Bachelors of Arts degree in Social

Science. I was so proud of myself for finishing college. Once I graduated I would be able to enroll in a teacher credentialing program and I'd be on my way to working in a public school and earning enough money to support myself. Then I could divorce Parrish and get on with my life.

I had decided about a year earlier that once I got my degree I would confront Parrish and give him the ultimatum; either he went to counseling with me or I would leave. I betted on him telling me to leave and I was prepared to do just that. In fact, one day while I was writing a paper for school, I actually packed up a bag of clothes and toiletries, grabbed my pillow, got in my car and left, heading to a friend's house. As I was driving I realized that I didn't bring my computer or any of my files along and I desperately needed to finish my classes. I turned around and went back home. Parrish never even noticed I left.

I graduated from college and threw myself a graduation party the following weekend to celebrate. All my friends were there and it dawned on me that I had a great support system. Even though Parrish didn't value me, plenty of others did. I knew I'd make it if he chose not to go to counseling with me.

Two days after my graduation party, we were right back in the flow of things and hosted our leadership Bible study on Monday night. When all the students had left, Parrish and I walked to our truck to head home. As I climbed into my seat, I saw a familiar car screeching around the corner and come to a stop across the street from us. The mom of the student I tutored jumped out of her vehicle and confronted Parrish before he could get in the truck.

"I need to talk to you and I don't think Mishell should hear it." She walked to the back of the truck, while Parrish followed leaving his door open so I could hear the entire conversation.

"What do you need to talk about?" Parrish asked as though it was just any conversation. Not as though she obviously had something serious to discuss.

"What my son and his friend just told me... I can't believe what they said... I can't believe it's true... that you've been... touching them!"

"I love those two boys. I would never hurt them!" he replied. I noticed that he didn't deny what she said. She noticed too.

"So, you're not denying it? I can't believe you! We trusted you!" she stormed to her car and drove away.

My heart sank. My life was shattered. I knew we didn't have the perfect life, but I thought I knew my husband. If he could do what she said to those boys, then I didn't know him at all.

Parrish eventually climbed back into the truck. I stared out the window as he drove us home, not sure how to start the conversation, but I had to know if he did it. I mustered the courage to ask, "Did you do what she says you did?"

"It's not like that. I love those boys." As though he was remembering a fond memory.

I couldn't fathom who this person driving me home was. Who could do what he was accused of, to junior high boys, or any child for that matter? I was married to a monster! "You molested them?" I managed to get the words out of my head and into the open where it sounded even worse.

"It's not like that. I love them. I wouldn't hurt them." He repeated the words he had told the mom minutes earlier.

I was shocked beyond comprehension. I couldn't even begin to wrap my head around what he did to those boys. Not just one boy, at least two. What else didn't I know? How did this happen? How did I not see it? Where did he do it? Was I there? How long has this been going on? How was I so clueless?

Never-ending questions bombarded me all the way home. The half-hour drive seemed to take forever, yet somehow, before I knew it, Parrish was directing the truck down our driveway. I walked into the house in a daze, not even acknowledging that he was there. I went about getting ready for bed in a fog and climbed under the covers, silently hoping that I could wake up in the morning to find that this was all just a huge misunderstanding.

Not long after I crawled under the blankets, Parrish climbed into bed beside me. I bristled as he rolled towards me and wrapped one arm around me pulling me into him. We hadn't slept in the same bed in months and this was the night he chose to end that! I was paralyzed, I didn't have the energy to pull away from him. I had wanted this affection from him, but not under these circumstances. He fell asleep easily and rolled away from me. I had a difficult time lying in bed next to him. I didn't want to sleep beside a monster. I contemplated sleeping on the couch, as he had been doing, but decided I was not going to allow this monster to take my bed away. He would not be sleeping with me after that night.

The next morning, we went about our routines. I found him in the bathroom, shaving, "I guess wishing you a happy birthday would be pretty ridiculous." It was his twenty-seventh birthday.

"I can fix this. I know their moms won't talk to me, but maybe they'll talk to you." He began. I could tell he had a plan and was going to make me a part of it. "Can you call Renee today and see if we can meet her for dinner. I'm sure if I can just explain what happened she'll understand."

"You want me to help you fix your problem?" I didn't want to help him, at the moment, I didn't even like him all that much.

"Yes please." He begged. "All you have to do is call her and set up a time for us to meet with her. If you love me, you'll do this one thing for me. Please!"

I couldn't help it. As much as he disgusted me, he was my husband and until I knew for sure what happened with those boys, I needed to stick by him. God would want me to be the loving supportive wife, no matter what.

"Fine." I replied. "I will make one phone call, but that's it."

"Thank you." He tried to hug me, but I pulled away. He was too distracted to notice.

We finished getting ready for work in relative silence and drove away in our separate trucks. All I could do was hope that what they accused him of was false. I didn't know what would happen to me, the boys, or Parrish if he had molested them.

On my first break of the morning, I walked to the school office so I could use the phone to try to call the mom at work and set up a meeting for that evening. She didn't answer the phone; it went straight to voicemail.

I hung up and immediately called Parrish at work.

"Hello, Mishell?" He answered.

"Hello." I was not friendly. "I can't get ahold of her. You're not going to get to meet with her."

"They're here. All of them, the parents and the kids, telling the pastor and the principal what I did. You have to come. I need you." He sounded like a frightened child, in need of comfort, saying the words that I had wanted to hear so many times before, but not now.

"I'll see what I can do. Bye." With that I hung up on him.

My principal had been standing there and knew that something was wrong. She agreed to make sure my class was covered for the rest of the day if I needed to leave. I drove straight to Parrish's school and walked directly to his office. The secretaries looked at me strangely as I passed them without saying a word. I didn't know how much they knew about what was going on, but I was sure they knew something.

I closed the door to his office after entering and stood facing him across his desk. "Well, I'm here. Now what?"

"I have to leave. I packed a bag of clothes this morning, it's in my truck. I have some money too. I'm going to drive to the beach, leave my wallet and keys in the truck and disappear."

"You are not leaving me here alone to deal with this mess you created! You can leave right now, with me, but we will be going home! You will not disappear! You will deal with this!" It felt good to stand up to him. I had been taught that according to the Bible, the wife was to be submissive to her husband so I always did what he wanted.

"We can leave now. They don't want me here anyway." He hung his head as though he was actually ashamed.

"You drive your truck home and I'll follow you and you better go straight home." I was livid. I couldn't believe he had thought to run away from this and leave me here alone to deal with the fallout. I had absolutely no idea what would happen, but I knew he had to face the consequences of his actions.

By the time we arrived home, there was a message on the answering machine from his principal asking him to not come back to work.

Our house was on the same property as Parrish's grandma and mom. When they saw that we were home in the middle of the day they came over to check on us. I sat by as he told his family what he was being accused of. I asked them to keep an eye on him for the rest of the week as I had to go back to work and I didn't want him to try to run away again.

It took a week living in a fog and not knowing what the future held before he was arrested. I was in the middle of teaching my class when I found out. My principal agreed to cover my class so I could go home where I found sheriff deputies waiting in my driveway to serve a search warrant for our house.

When the sheriffs completed their search, I packed a bag and headed to Kim's house, she had been a friend ever since she made my wedding cake. I spent the next few months sleeping on her couch and working at getting the shattered pieces of my life back together.

Chapter Thirty

I was married to a child molester. Everything about my life had been a lie. I was a shattered. The divorce had been inevitable, but finding out that Parrish was a monster shook me to the core.

I knew he and I had issues, but I had no clue that was molesting children. I was suddenly thankful that we hadn't had children. I had been with Parrish for seven and a half years and I obviously didn't know him. He had been excellent at keeping that part of himself hidden from me. I didn't know how I would trust anyone ever again.

During this horrific time in my life, I realized who my true friends were; the ones who were there for me through thick and thin. Many people left my side, either because they believed that Parrish was innocent of the accusations, they believed I knew what was happening and did nothing to stop it, or they were too scared to confront the reality that a friend of theirs could be a child molester. I prefer to think the latter was true, I didn't want anyone to believe that I knew about the abuse and did nothing. I was so involved in my life that I didn't see what Parrish was hiding so well in his.

Kim and her husband Jeff became my best friends. They allowed me to sleep on their couch for months and listen to me talk through my emotions. They attended every court date with me. Kim made sure that I ate three meals every day. Jeff and Kim even tricked me into seeing a counselor. I don't think I would have survived those first months of my new life without them.

Even though I believed Parrish did what he was accused of, even though I believed he was the monster the boys said he was, even though he completely disgusted me, I had to go visit him in jail twice a week every week. Even though I was currently sleeping on Jeff and Kim's couch, my house was still on his family property. That meant that until I had removed all my belongings from my house, I had to pretend that all was well with Parrish and me so I would be able to maintain access to my house.

I visited him in jail twice a week throughout the summer and even after I started back to work in the fall. I learned more than I ever wanted to know about visiting an inmate. You aren't allowed to wear shorts, tank tops, or anything that reveals too much skin. You had to pass through a metal detector and have your driver's license or other government issued identification. Visits were on the hour for fifty minutes and you had to be checked in at least a half an hour prior to the visit start time. You were assigned a visiting room and when you're finally allowed in the room, you must wait for the prisoner to be brought in on their side. A thick glass divides you from the inmate and you communicate through a phone receiver.

Every visit with him was difficult, but we talked more to each other while he was in jail than we had talked in the previous few years. I pretended to be the supportive wife, telling him what he wanted to hear, that I'd stay with him and we'd get through this together. I asked him questions about what he did, I never showed him how angry or disgusted I was with him.

Through these visits, he revealed that he had carried on a physical relationship with a former youth pastor of ours for the entire length of our marriage. I discovered love letters that he had hidden at our house, to a boy when he was in high school. I confronted him about that in one of our visits and discovered that he had feelings for this boy and his family didn't want him to be gay so he started dating me to show them that he was straight.

While I was visiting him on a regular basis, I was also making a plan for my future. I would not stay married to him, so I found a divorce lawyer. I found my own apartment and moved all my belongings out of the house we had shared on his family property for the past three years. I will always remember the last visit I had with him in December of 1999.

I watched as Parrish entered the visitor room and picked up the receiver on his side. "Hey Mishell. Thanks for coming." He began the same as all our previous visits.

"Hi." I cleared my voice before continuing. "I want to let you know that this is the last time I will be visiting you. I have my own place now and I'll be moving out of our house."

"What? Why? You promised you'd stay with me through this." He sounded confused and a little whiny.

"I lied to you. Just like you did when you married me. This is the last time I'll visit you. I have an appointment with a divorce lawyer this week. Good bye." I placed the receiver back in its cradle, stood up, turned away from Parrish and walked out the door, never looking back.

It was the beginning of a new life for me. New words filled my mind.

Strong.
Brave.
Smart.
Enough.
Valuable.
I was worthless no more.

Chapter Thirty-One

My last visit with Parrish was extremely satisfying. I had spent my entire life making choices and doing things to keep the people around me happy and I was done doing that. The next chapter of my life would be for me. I would figure out who I was and what I wanted out of life and do it. I would no longer live just to please others, nobody would control me again.

I continued to attend church with Kim and Jeff as well as see my counselor at least once a week. There were also many conversations with God in the living room of my very own, one-bedroom apartment. It was a difficult, but rewarding time in my life.

I was single for the first time in ten years. I had begun dating Jay when just shy of my fifteenth birthday, went straight from him to dating Paul. Then from Paul I jumped into a relationship with Parrish. In those ten years, two out of three relationships weren't good for me; I was physically, sexually, emotionally and spiritually abused by two men who were supposed to be good Christians. The only boyfriend I had in that time that treated me with any respect was Paul and he hadn't been a Christian. Was dating a Christian really what God required?

As a newly single person, I needed to decide if I even wanted another relationship, if I could trust a person enough to get that close to again and if I would date only Christians or not make that a priority in future relationships. I was only twenty-five years old and didn't want to spend the rest of my life alone, so I would need to learn to trust again so that I could have a healthy, solid relationship. That was going to take a lot of work with my counselor and God.

I didn't trust myself to be a good judge of character. I had dated two people, and married one of them, that I had thought were decent human beings. I especially thought that when Parrish decided to become a youth pastor, but I had no idea what kind of monster was hidden within the depths of his soul. It made me hesitant to trust myself to choose a good person, how would I know if they were who they portrayed themselves to be?

Being the rational, list and detail person that I am, I wanted to learn as much as I could about dating and relationships. I talked to my counselor at length about what makes a healthy, long-lasting relationship and how I could trust someone enough to allow them into my heart. I read books about dating, one that was extremely helpful was *Boundaries in Dating* by Dr. Henry Cloud and Dr. John Townsend. That book made me see that it is possible to know what you want in a relationship and not settle for somebody who offers you less than what you expect.

I still struggled with the idea that God only wanted me to date a Christian when the only person I had dated that treated me with respect had not been a Christian. I also struggled with how God could have a plan for my life when I was used goods. I was somebody else's thrown away wife. Who could love me now? How could God love me when I divorced my husband? I had learned at a young age that God hated divorce and that all marriages could be saved. It's the reason that my mom never divorced my dad, even though they lived separate for most of my life; my mom didn't want to upset God by divorcing my dad.

Who was I that God would forgive me for disrespecting my husband by divorcing him? I studied the Bible for myself and learned on my own that abuse or abandonment were perfectly acceptable, Biblical reasons to get a divorce. If how Parrish had treated me during our relationship and if molesting those boys wasn't abusive and if being arrested wasn't abandoning me then I would happily go to hell for divorcing him. I began to feel confident in my decision to divorce him and that I could be happily married again.

With the help of the Bible, dating books and my counseling sessions, I learned that the most important aspect of having a strong, healthy and happy relationship is to be mentally and emotionally strong, healthy and happy not being in a relationship. That was a huge breakthrough as I had spent most my life defining my worth by being in a relationship with my parents or with boys. I needed to know my value on my own before anybody else would be able to see my value.

I cried to God, to Kim, to my counselor and in the pages of my journal as I wrote about my struggles with self-worth. In the midst of the crying, talking and writing I also listened and learned that I was created by God as a unique human being and that there was no person on this earth who was exactly the same as me. This revelation was easier to learn than to put into action in my life, but slowly I did. I grew more confident and started to be happy with myself, my life and the choices I was making.

The most freeing life lesson I learned through almost a year of soul searching was that the way other people treated me reflected who they were as a person, it was not a reflection of me. Their actions affected my life, but the choices they made were theirs alone and had nothing to do with me. I was a valuable human being no matter how other people treated me.

Once I learned these life lessons, knew I was valuable and was happy being me, I decided I was ready to start dating again. This time I wanted to do it right. I didn't want to waste time on someone that wasn't right for me or didn't treat me the way I deserved to be treated. Like the book had taught me, I needed boundaries in my next relationship. I also wanted to have an idea beforehand of the kind of man I would marry someday, so I made a list of the things I wanted in my next partner and what things would be red flags in the relationship.

Things my next partner must have:

> A lifted 4x4 truck
>
> good money management   goals
>
> A relationship with God   respect
> communication skills
>
> Honesty   integrity
> reliable job
>
> Faithfulness   no drugs
> no alcoholism

Red flags that would end a relationship:

> Disrespecting me   liking boys
> tons of debt
>
> Current drug use   alcohol abuse
> lying

It wasn't an exhaustive list, but it was a glimpse at what I was looking for in a future partner. I wanted to be able to meet somebody, find these things out about them and make a decision about continuing the relationship before I developed real feelings for them; I didn't want to waste my time. Besides the fact that I was twenty-five years old, I had been accepted into San Diego State University's teacher credential program and would be moving there at the end of the summer. If I met someone before I moved, I would need to know if they were worth pursuing for a long-distance relationship, so I created the list.

Chapter Thirty-Two

A few months after I wrote my list of characteristics for my future partner, school got out and I got a job working at a local Italian deli. I had worked there off and on over the years of my marriage to Parrish, the owner there was incredible and let me work when I needed to earn extra money or was out of school. I met a lot of people while working there, one liked car racing so we talked quite a bit.

This guy liked racecars so much that he volunteered at a local racetrack on Saturday nights on the fire crew. They are the ones that respond to wrecks on the track and make sure that the cars don't get destroyed by fire. During one of our many conversations while I served him homemade raviolis, he asked if I'd like to join the fire crew. I was nervous at first because I had never been that close to cars driving that fast, but I eventually said yes and I'm so glad I did.

There were four guys on the fire crew and I was the only girl. I liked the odds, but I wasn't expecting to meet Mr. Right out there. The first night that I volunteered, I had to go straight from working at the deli to the racetrack, so I packed up some of the leftover food and took it with me to share with the guys on the crew. I was in, they absolutely loved me, or my food, whatever, and I was part of a new group.

Every Saturday night, I would leave work and bring food out to the guys. The fire crew wore fluorescent green shirts and stood on a podium in the middle of the track so that we were close to the action and could always see what was going on. There was another group of volunteers, the safety crew, who wore safety orange t-shirts and were there to clean up any debris after a wreck. One week, two of the safety crew members came over to talk to one of the fire crew members. I couldn't tell you what one of them looked like, but the other one was blond, with blue eyes and a medium build. He reminded me of Owen Wilson, a popular actor at the time. I was introduced to both of them, but I only remember the blond one's name, Mike.

Each week after that I would try to catch a glimpse of Mike as I walked across the track to take my place on the podium. A few weeks after that first introduction I didn't see him in his usual position on the track with the rest of the safety crew, I was a little disappointed. That was short-lived however, because when I drew closer to the podium, he was standing there in a fluorescent green fire crew shirt. He was working with us that night and I would finally have a chance to talk to him.

We talked off and on between races and wrecks and learned that we had a lot in common. He liked fast cars, so did I, we both played bass guitar in our church worship bands, and we knew a lot of the same people. He played in the worship band at his church with some of the people I knew from youth group when I was in high school. We even knew the same person that had won a classic Mustang! It was a small world.

A few weeks later, on a Sunday night, I decided to attend his church to see him play in the band. As soon as the pastor said "amen" ending the service that evening, Mike made a beeline straight to me. It was as if nobody else existed in the entire building except him and me. He singled me out and we talked while I followed him onstage to pack up all his gear, then we walked out to the parking lot together.

We stood and talked in the parking lot for at least forty-five minutes. We discussed so many things, the entire time my thoughts were running through my list. He was a member of the worship team, so he had a relationship with God. We were standing next to his lifted, 4x4 truck; check. He had a job and was in training to become an electrician, so he had goals. He met enough of my criteria that if he asked me for a date, I would accept without reservation.

It was getting late as we stood there talking and I needed to get home. "I hate to do this to you, but I need to leave."

"Where're you parked? I'll walk you to your car." He offered.

"Just over here." I thought that he was finally going to ask me out as we walked towards my car. "Well, here we are." I unlocked my car and opened the door.

"Okay." He fidgeted. "Drive safe."

"Alright. Good night." I was confused. We had been talking for about an hour, couldn't he see that I was interested?

"Good night." He said before turning to walk back to his truck.

I got into my car, closed the door and turned the key in the ignition, the engine came to life. When I turned around to check behind me so I could back out and head home, I saw Mike walking back towards my car. I left the car running, but got out to see what he wanted.

"Would you want to go to dinner and a movie with me sometime?" He asked as soon as I got out of the car.

"Yes, I would. When do you want to do it?" I wasn't leaving now without an actual date planned.

"I'm free Wednesday. Would that work?" He asked.

"That'd be perfect. I work until six. Can you pick me up at seven?" I wanted all the details hashed out now.

"Sounds good. Can I get your number and address?"

"Of course you can." I dug around in my car for a pen and paper. When my search was successful, I wrote my information down and gave it to him. "Now, I really have to go. Good night. See you Wednesday." A smile spread across my face like I hadn't experienced in years.

I climbed back inside my car and drove home in a happy daze. I had a date with a handsome young man who I just happened to have a lot in common with. Wednesday was only three days away, but it seemed like an eternity.

When the big night finally arrived, I raced home from work and jumped into the shower to wash away the smell of garlic and raviolis. Then I must have tried on at least a dozen outfits before deciding on a simple denim skirt and white, collared t-shirt with a pair of sandals. To say I was nervous would be putting it mildly, I was pacing around the house while I waited for him to show up. I went over my list with my roommate to see how I could fit some of the topics into dinner conversation.

My heart skipped a few beats and my breath caught in my throat when Mike rang the doorbell to pick me up. I tried not to show how excited I was; I didn't want to seem anxious to him. My friend opened the door and welcomed Mike into the house. After I introduced them, he and I walked out the door to his truck.

He rushed ahead of me and opened the passenger's door for me. "Let me get that for you."

"Thank you." I had to climb into his lifted truck in a mini-skirt without flashing him while he was being a gentleman and held the door open for me. It was a sweet gesture, but it was difficult to maintain my dignity. I think I was successful in not giving him a show, at least he never said anything.

He walked around the truck and opened the driver's door, reaching behind the seat, he pulled out a single red rose and handed it to me. "I got this for you. I hope you like it."

"It's beautiful!" I was glad it was just a single rose since I was allergic to them and didn't want to ruin the evening with an allergy attack. I also didn't want to make him feel bad for such a nice gesture so I didn't tell him I was allergic. "So where are we going for dinner?"

"I was thinking about this restaurant called 'Waterloo,' one of the guys at work said it's good."

"I've never been there, but I've heard it's good too." I had wanted to try that restaurant, but Parrish never took me. I was excited to finally get to try it out with good company.

We talked as we drove to the restaurant and throughout dinner, he showed me a picture of his one-year old niece and he told me about his best friend's wedding that he was going to be the best man in coming up the next weekend. I asked him as many questions as I could to find out how many things on my list he could check off. I'm sure he felt like he was at a long, drawn out interview instead of on a date, but I wanted to know if I should have a second date, especially since I was moving to San Diego for school six weeks after our date. After dinner, we went for ice cream and to see a movie. At the end of the date he walked me to the door and we awkwardly hugged as we said good night.

I went into my room and pulled out the list. I could tick off enough boxes with what I learned about him on the date that if he asked for another date I would have said yes. I needed to find out about the red flag side of the list too. I waited and waited and waited for a phone call for a second date. After his friend's wedding, he finally called me and asked me to go to Santa Cruz with him for the Fourth of July. Of course, I accepted the invitation, I wanted to spend as much time as I possibly could with him to get to know more about him.

On Tuesday morning, the Fourth of July, I woke up early to get ready for my second date with Mike. He showed up right on time and we climbed into his truck for the two-and-a-half-hour drive to Santa Cruz. I continued asking him questions, to see how many more requirements from my list he fulfilled, as well as to find out more about him and his family. We shopped on the wharf, ate lunch at the Boardwalk and rode as many roller coasters as we could fit into the day.

When evening came and the sun set over the horizon, casting amazing shades of red, orange and pink across the ocean, we took a walk along the beach where the water just licks the seashore. When I looked behind us, I could see our footprints in the sand, side by side. When the sun had been down for about thirty minutes, fireworks began to light up the night sky.

I stood beside Mike, watching the fireworks in awe that it was the day that I was finally free. Independence Day was the day that my divorce from Parrish became official. It seemed that the fireworks exploding in the sky were celebrating my freedom, my value and my importance. Nobody else knew the celebration was just for me, Mike didn't even know, but it was.

After the grand finale, Mike and I turned away from the beach and headed back towards the lights of the Boardwalk to head home for the night. As we walked, I kept bumping into him, not on purpose, but we were so close together and walking a straight line in the sand is hard.

About halfway back to the Boardwalk, he reached for my hand and laced his fingers through mine. "This should keep you from bumping into me so much." He laughed.

I laughed too, "I doubt it." We walked hand in hand all the way back to his truck, with me continuing to bump into him. It was incredibly sweet.

He took me back to Santa Cruz a few weeks later to celebrate my twenty-sixth birthday. He surprised me with a picnic on the beach. He had a blanket, dinner and even a tiny birthday cake. We sat on the beach, enjoying the food and the view of the moon reflecting in the water and the sound of the waves crashing on the beach.

When we were done enjoying dinner and dessert, he reached into his bag and pulled out a gift. "This is for you. I hope you like it."

"Thank you!" I took it from his hands and tore at the paper. I gasped when I saw the gift. Inside the package was a watch with a leather band and a blue face with Bugs Bunny on it; his ears were the hands that moved around keeping the time. "I love it!" I reached across the space between us and wrapped my arms around his neck, planting a kiss on his lips.

He pulled away from my embrace, and took my hands in his. "I have something to tell you too. I love you." His eyes locked onto mine.

He loves me; he just told me he loves me! He really does love me! This watch proves that he listens to me and cares about me. I stayed quiet a moment longer letting that sink in. Then I saw a shadow of doubt pass across his face.

I needed to say something to him. "I love you too!" I meant it. He was everything on my list and so much more. He was a man of integrity and honesty, who genuinely cared about others, not just what they could do for him.

"I'm glad you said something. I was getting worried." We both laughed.

We sat on the beach for a bit longer and watched the reflection of the moon dancing on the water before we had to head home since both of us had to work the next day.

As the summer wore on, we saw each other every day and decided that we would keep this relationship going long distance when I moved to San Diego. A few times we even mentioned the idea of marriage. Then in mid-August, Mike helped me load up the few belonging that I had left and move into my dorm.

Chapter Thirty-Three

On Thursday of my first week living in San Diego I received a phone call.

"Hello." I answered when the phone rang.

"Hi, Mishell. It's Vicki," Mike's mom. "How are you?"

"Okay, I guess, getting used to it here." It was hard being so far away from everybody I knew, but I didn't want to worry her.

"Listen, I called because Mike is miserable without you here. I just bought a plane ticket for you to come home for the weekend. You need to pick it up at the airport tomorrow at four. I'll have Michael pick you up here."

"Are you serious? That's so great. Thank you so much." I didn't know what else to say, I was going to get to see Mike again.

She gave me all the details about the airline and times before we hung up. I immediately started to pack for the first of many weekends with Mike. Throughout the semester that I attended San Diego State, we spent almost every weekend together; either I went home or he drove down. Eventually our conversations turned to marriage. On one weekend when I went home his mom had a surprise for me.

After breakfast Saturday morning, she and I went dress shopping, not just for any old dress, but for wedding dresses. Mike hadn't asked me to marry him yet, but we had talked about marriage so I happily went along. We had appointments at a few stores and I tried on so many dresses that I lost count, but none of them were the right dress for me. We ended up at a dress store in town where I agreed to try on a few more dresses.

I picked out three or four dresses to take into the dressing, but the first one I tried on was it. As soon as I saw my reflection in the mirror I knew that it was the dress I would wear when I walked down the aisle to say "I do" to Mike. I walked out of the dressing room to show his mom, my friend, and the store worker. Everyone agreed, it was my dress.

Vicki offered to buy it for me, since I was an unemployed student. I wasn't even engaged yet, but I knew I needed that dress so I agreed.

Driving home later, Vicki turned to me at a stop light. "Your ring is absolutely beautiful!"

I looked down at my empty ring finger, "What ring?"

Her eyes grew wide as she followed my gaze down to my finger. "He hasn't proposed yet?"

"Not yet."

"Well he has the ring and it's beautiful. Please don't tell him I spoiled it." She seemed embarrassed.

"I'll act surprised." I promised.

I expected the proposal to happen that weekend, but it didn't happen that weekend or the next weekend or the one after that. I was beginning to think he had decided to wait until I moved back home and quit expecting it every time I saw him.

His birthday was in November, so I planned to come home for the weekend and take him to dinner to celebrate. I took him to Santa Cruz, where we had celebrated my birthday just a few months earlier.

I took him to a restaurant at the end of the wharf where we shared our two favorite meals; a bacon cheeseburger with fries and chicken fettuccini Alfredo. After dinner, we went for a walk ending up on the beach, where the waves had made the sand wet enough during high tide to make walking easy.

We walked and talked for a bit before Mike stopped walking and turned to face me. "I have something for you." He said, reaching into his coat pocket.

"Why do you have something for me? It's your birthday. I'm supposed to give you a gift." I was clueless.

"Please let me do this." He knelt down in the wet sand.

I gasped, my eyes grew wide and my hands flew over my mouth. I knew what he was going to do and I didn't want to ruin it.

He had a small box in his hand that he pulled from his pocket. He looked up at me from his kneeling position. "I love you with everything in me. Will you marry me?"

"Yes! Of course I'll marry you!" shaking I held out my hand for him to slip the engagement ring onto my finger, then we hugged.

He stood up, wiped the sand from his knee, and laced his fingers through mine. We walked across the sand to the arcade at the Boardwalk and took "engagement" pictures in a photo booth.

I had never been so happy in my entire life. I had no doubt that I was a valuable person and Mike knew it too.

I was getting married to an amazing man.

I had a terrible childhood, believing I was worthless and that my value as a human being could only be found in others. Now I knew my own worth, and so did my future husband. I was the luckiest girl in the world. New words flooded my mind.

Strong.
Healed.
Forgiven.
Whole.
Valuable.
Priceless.
Beautiful.
I was worthless no more.

Epilogue

My purpose for writing my story is to help others who may be going through a similar situation. I thought I was completely alone amid the turmoil that made up my young life. I didn't believe that anybody else could possibly be experiencing anything like I was. I know better now.

We all have different stories and different reactions to the events in our lives, but a whole lot of people have gone through situations that hurt, make them feel worthless and possibly suicidal. The abuser wants us to believe that we are alone, that there is nobody who can understand what we're going through or help us out of it. That is untrue!

If you have suffered any kind of abuse you need to talk to a trusted adult, if you are a minor, or a trusted friend. You need to report the abuse and allow the law to take care of your abuser. Then you need to forgive them so that you can begin your journey of healing and begin to write a new ending to your story.

Here are a few places you can go for help:

National Sexual Assault Hotline call 800-656-HOPE (4673) or go to www.rainn.org/

National Suicide Prevention Hotline call 1-800-273-8255 or text 'HELP' to 741741

Domestic Violence Hotline 1-800-799-SAFE (7233)

Your local law enforcement agency.

A trusted teacher, counselor, family member or co-worker.

Acknowledgements

There are many people whose stories intertwine with mine to make my story possible. Thank you all for the part you have played in my story.

God for taking the shattered pieces of my life and making me whole again.

My husband, Mike, for loving me through everything and supporting me in writing and publishing this book.

My kids, Aleigh and Aaron, for making me a mom and giving me a chance to do better for them.

Cindy, Stefyni, and Keeth for being the best siblings and giving me so many great memories.

Kim Etcheverry whose story intertwines with mine in so many places.

Pastor Tim for showing me the true nature of God.

My in-laws for giving me the family I always needed.

Paul and his parents who loved me when I didn't love myself and showed me a glimpse of how life should be.

Daisy Rain Martin for letting me know that it's my story to tell.

Hailey Anderson, Sorrel Gonzalez, and Sundus Khan for reading my story and giving suggestions for making my book a better read.

All my students for being awesome and listening to my story. Have fun! Be safe! Make good choices!

About the Author

Mishell Wolff is a teacher and author living with her husband, two kids, two turtles and dog in the Northern Central Valley of California. After surviving a controlling family and a couple of abusive relationships, she is happily married to a wonderful man. They have two amazing children who keep them extremely busy.
Follow her on social media
Facebook: Mishell Wolff
Read her weekly blog and stay updated on future books on her website: mishellwolff.com

www.ingramcontent.com/pod-product-compliance
Lightning Source LLC
Chambersburg PA
CBHW070603300426
44113CB00010B/1386